THE
U.S.
SENATE

ALSO BY GEORGE E. REEDY

THE
U.S.
SENATE

*Paralysis or a Search
for Consensus?*

BY GEORGE E. REEDY

CROWN PUBLISHERS, INC.
New York

This book is dedicated with affection
and a touch of nostalgia to the ablest group of people
with whom I have ever worked—the 1950s staff
of the Senate Democratic Policy Committee.
In addition to my personal assistant Willie Day Taylor,
they included Roland H. Bibolet, Isabel Brown, Solis Horwitz,
Bill Lloyd, Harry McPherson, Pauline Moore, Gerry Siegel,
Grace Tully, Jim Wilson and Marie Wilson—names which
deserve public recognition somewhere for their selfless service
to a fundamental American institution.
I am very proud to have been associated with them.

Copyright © 1986 by George E. Reedy
Published by Crown Publishers, Inc.,
225 Park Avenue South, New York, New York 10003
and represented in Canada by the Canadian MANDA Group.
CROWN is a trademark of Crown Publishers, Inc.
Manufactured in the United States of America
Library of Congress Cataloging-in-Publication Data
Reedy, George E., 1917–
    The U.S. Senate.
    Includes index.
    1. United States. Congresses. Senate.
I. Title.
JK1170.R44 1986   328.73'07   86-8906
ISBN 0-517-56239-1
10 9 8 7 6 5 4 3 2 1
First Edition

Contents

1. Senate Anonymous   1
2. A Body That Does Nothing   21
3. The Fine Art of Voting   38
4. Prelude of Frustration   47
5. To a Worldwide Role   64
6. The Cast of Characters   85
7. Building Unity   100
8. The Coalition Under a Microscope   113
9. Lines of Strategy Form   129
10. Preliminary Maneuvering   146
11. Back in the Majority   159
12. The Pride That Goeth Before the Fall   175
13. What Price Efficiency?   190
14. The Center Cannot Hold   202
    Acknowledgments   214
    Index   215

222786

1

Senate Anonymous

It is something of a commentary on the American political system that my name, to the extent that it is known outside of my circle of friends, is associated with the White House. People who are not quite certain whether they have seen me on television or on the Post Office wall stop me on the street and say: "Aren't you that fellow who was in Washington with Kennedy or Johnson?" Total strangers, meeting me for the first time, will say: "You're the Presidential man in Milwaukee. Who's going to win the nomination?" I do not wish to leave the impression that my rounds of the city find me constantly besieged by such people. Like that of a former Vice President, my name is hardly a household word. But there are enough such incidents to prove my point. Any association with the Presidency creates a limited form of immortality—at least for a couple of decades.

To me, there is a certain irony in such recognition. My span in the White House was relatively brief and I do not regard myself as having performed any service of tremendous merit during that time. I was surrounded by "doers," all of whom were intent on doing things I thought had better been left undone. Unfortunately, the activists were more in tune with the President than I and I could do little more than be an observer. In later years, a columnist reviewing my book *The Twilight of the Presidency* remarked that I was like "the plain girl at the party" who did no dancing but who saw and noted everything that happened. The description may have been apt.

My more interesting life in Washington—at least to me—was spent around the Senate, either as a journalist or an aide. This, in my mind, is the most fascinating of all governmental institutions. It is a body of subtlety, of grace, of flexibility. It has the capacity to discriminate between winds of social change and temporary gusts that will leave no lasting impression. When there is a genuine emergency, it can act with bewildering speed. But there are other times when it can dawdle with a frustrating indifference to the urgings of partisans. Above all, it is a purely political organism that reflects, with a high degree of verisimilitude, the political realities of democracy in the United States. It is our most representative institution.

The last point requires some explaining. If one thinks of representative democracy solely in terms of the "one man, one vote" theory, the Senate is nowhere near it. The House of Representatives comes closer to playing that role, however imperfect may be the performance. But if one thinks of representative government as offering parallels to the social, economic, and political power relations within the nation, the Senate is obviously the model. Without the constant prodding of the House, it would have a tendency to freeze our society. But it has a saving grace. It can change as the power relationships in society change and it can do so more easily than other governmental institutions that, at least in theory, are closer to the "grass roots."

Incidentally, I hope no one assumes that I am denigrating the House of Representatives. It is a body with considerable charm and its members are rarely stuffy. It is by far the best barometer of the collective mood of the country at any given moment even though it is not very good at forecasting the direction in which it is going. It is politics of the bare-knuckled variety—thumb-in-the-eye, knee-in-the-groin—and it is fun to watch. As a reporter, I enjoyed covering the House much more than I did the Senate, which can exude an institutional pomposity that is excruciating. To this day, I cringe inwardly when I hear the words "great debate," which invariably foreshadow weeks of platitudinous orotundities and impassioned obfuscation (I am picking this language deliberately because that's the way the speeches sound). No Senator would ever try to bring a pig onto the floor, as one House member tried to do during consideration of a bill.

What must be understood, however, is that pomposity in the Senate serves a purpose. It provides the time for the extended maneuvering and sharp bargaining that leads to incredibly subtle compromises. Whoever originated the idea that Senate debate is "educational" for the public was either ignorant of the educational process or had never heard the speeches. But as long as somebody on the Senate floor is talking, the Senate cannot vote and the

Senate leaders can use the time provided to work out the necessary legislative compromises. Whenever Lyndon B. Johnson needed extra time for horse trading and a vote was inconveniently near, he invariably sent out for Hubert H. Humphrey, who could stand up and deliver a discourse ranging from two to ten hours without previous preparation.

In the House of Representatives, the time for debate is strictly limited. This is one of the factors that determine the character of the institution. Compromises are rarely reached on the floor and legislative consideration of a bill has the coloration of a showdown battle between forces that are determined to annihilate each other. Measures are either passed or defeated or amended so drastically as to amount to a defeat. It is rare (I cannot think of an instance) that the members reach the Senate type of compromise in which the minority can comfort itself by some form of recognition of its importance.

It is this latter quality that has brought about my long-standing love affair with the Senate. At the conclusion of a House debate, the losers are left with little comfort and no political weapons other than yammering. The final vote always comes in the form of "sudden death" and I have often wondered whether it would not be appropriate to signal that fact by blowing the *deguillado*—the Spanish bugle call that tells the attackers to slaughter all of the opposing soldiers and to take no prisoners. Such an outcome is satisfying to the winners, who believe that justice has triumphed. But I have some doubts as to the life span of a democratic nation that would ground its legislative production on principles of partisan justice. It is the Senate that provides the cushions against the shocks of political defeat and thereby enables the minority to maintain a viable relationship with the majority. I do not believe that the United States could have sustained its unity over so many decades without the Senate.

Despite its importance, however, the Senate, of all our institutions, is probably the least understood by the great mass of the American people. This is not at all surprising. We usually understand whatever is outside our area of personal experience by drawing parallels to those phenomena that are within that area. Where the parallels are valid, this form of thought is quite adequate. Unfortunately, there is nothing within the life of most citizens that affords a valid parallel. They can understand the Presidency in terms of the authority figures in their own existence—father, teacher, lawman, or boss. They can understand the House of Representatives in terms of other deliberative bodies with whom they do have direct contact—union committees, school boards, city councils, rural cooperatives. But none of these entities operate in the manner of the Senate. They are designed for yes or no responses to issues and such answers are not the goals of the Senate. There are very few of us who encounter in our everyday lives a force that controls and reflects social change with a desire to soften the heavier blows for those who are going to be hurt (all social change, no matter how essential, hurts somebody) and whose fundamental purpose is sustaining national unity.

Under the circumstances, most of the people I meet have shaped their view of the Senate out of its most obvious *public* characteristic—talk. Those who are kindly disposed toward the body view it as an arena in which orators discuss the great issues of the day in order to reach

5

prudent conclusions in the public interest. It is terribly disillusioning for those who have such a picture to visit the nation's Capitol Building and find that most of the speeches are made in a chamber that is almost empty except for the employees who must be on the floor during a session. It is not at all surprising that those who have gone through this experience leap to the conclusion that Senators are paid for windbaggery. Of course, the Capitol guides explain to the visitors they are bringing through the galleries that the floor is empty because "most of the work is done in committees." The explanation is unconvincing simply because it is untrue. Committees, except for Appropriations, must have a special dispensation to meet during a session of the Senate. But what the members are really doing cannot be explained in a few brief sentences to a general audience on a guided tour. The reality is far too subtle and I will be fortunate if I can begin to explain it in an entire book.

Until recently, the great bulk of academic literature on the Senate was not much better. This is due in part to the influence of Woodrow Wilson's book on the American Congress and in part to the evolutionary development of the body into an institution far different from that envisaged by the Founding Fathers. Wilson was a great admirer of the British Parliament and faulted the American legislature because it did not behave like the House of Commons and the House of Lords. Because he was the first academic to "make it" in big-time politics, his views carried more weight than they deserved. As for the Founding Fathers, they instituted the Senate as a means of securing approval of the Constitution by small states who feared that they would be swamped by large states if the only basis for legislative apportionment was population. (Of course, the Founding Fathers, most of whom were aristocrats, also expected the Senate to act as a check on the excesses of pure democracy. But, as we shall see, the reality has gone many miles from the starting point.)

Journalism, both print and electronic, adds to the widespread misunderstanding of the nature of the Senate. This is not due to any lack of will on the part of correspondents but to the nature of their profession. The purpose of journalism is to give us a daily account of visible *events,* and where events are central to the goals of an institution, journalistic conventions work quite well. Events are *not* central to the character of the Senate—or at least the kind of events that are amenable to measurement. Subtle shifts in thought; minute modifications in language that are intended to increase palatability; the quick formation of ad hoc blocs and their rapid dissolution are matters that do not lend themselves to block paragraphs. The process is comparable to giving daily news coverage of a chess match to an audience whose intellectual games experience has been limited to tic-tac-toe.

The dilemma created for newspaper reporters by this situation is frustrating. They *know* that what happens in the Senate is important to the American people. They *must* cover the body even though they are not geared to such coverage. Therefore, their tendency is to report pseudo-events—actions that are of little real importance but that do fit into the "who, what, when, how, and why" formula pounded into student heads in introductory journalism courses. It should be added that the formula works quite well in explaining the *content* of legislative enactments but not in explaining the machinery that brought it about.

I felt the frustration of journalism in my first brush with

the United States Senate in the fall of 1939. The United Press had placed me on its Senate staff to cover the special session called by Franklin Delano Roosevelt to amend the Neutrality Act. It was a choice plum for a youngster who had just turned twenty-two and whose previous experience had consisted of covering police in Philadelphia and providing vacation relief for regular reporters in secondary governmental agencies. I was excited at the thought of covering what had been advertised as a "great debate" and looked forward to oratory that would be an intellectual treat. There could be no doubt about the importance of the session. For two decades, the United States had been surrounding itself with walls of isolation intended to insulate us from European wars. Now Europe had again been plunged into war and the President was proposing to tear down one of those walls so we could take sides. The issue was of Homeric dimensions.

I quickly discovered, however, that the speeches did not live up to the issue. After the first few days, they became dull, repetitive, pompous, and generally irrelevant. The wire services were required to have a representative in the press gallery at all times during a session and this assignment was handed out to staff members in the same spirit that the army places its men on kitchen police. I can still recall one of my fellow sufferers saying to me, under his breath: "God, what I'd give for a chance to go out and cover a fire right now—something that was real." Senator Charles Tobey, of New Hampshire, who was opposed to the President, offered a procedural amendment to split the final vote into two parts. There was no chance that it would carry and it was doubtful whether it would have made any difference if it had. But it provided an "event" and we persuaded ourselves that the event was important. For two or three days we managed to stay on the front pages by billing the amendment as a major test of administration strength. When it was finally defeated—a result as predictable as the sunrise—we were left with nothing to write but meaninglss polls of the Senate—meaningless because it was already apparent that the bill would pass. For journalists, the final vote was an act of mercy putting them out of their misery.

And yet, it was perfectly clear to anyone of sensitivity in contact with the Senate on a daily basis that fascinating shifts were taking place. The pro-administration Senators were hardening in their resolve to help the British and the French even though none of them, at that point, were ready to intervene militarily or even economically. The anti-administration Senators, on the other hand, were in the process of evolving a theory that Nazi victory was inevitable and that the United States was in danger of being drawn in on the losing side because of "internal" (meaning Jewish) political pressures. Unfortunately, none of this came to us in a recordable form. The pro-administration Senators could not justly be called war hawks, although that is what many of them later became; the isolationists could not justly be called Nazi sympathizers, although some of them skirted dangerously close to that position. What we were picking up came to us in the form of individual conversations at lunch, while walking down corridors, or over quiet drinks at the Carroll Arms bar. Furthermore, no Senator stated it in the manner of this paragraph. The shift could be detected only by putting nonconnected conversations together. Had I attempted to submit any of this as a story, I would have received a sharp reminder that my business was to report "facts" rather than "impressions."

Unfortunately, the impressions were more important than the facts. The *passage* of the bill did little more than signal the British and the French that we were flexible. But the *process* of passage paved the way for open intervention at a later point. Had Roosevelt started out by proposing intervention on the side of the Allies, he would have been defeated without question. The neutrality bill, however, launched an intellectual course, glacially slow but just as inexorable, which eventually led to our open participation in the war against the Axis powers. As a journalist, I could see what was happening but had no method of conveying my important knowledge to my audience. All I could put on paper consisted of nonessentials.

The experience gave me no clues as to how journalists *could* cover the Senate in a manner that would be meaningful to the American people. Forty-five years later, I have come to the realization that the problem does not lie with journalists but with the public. The basic assumption of journalism is that it supplies facts to an audience that is educated to a point where it can use them. When the subject matter of the facts is outside the ken of the journalistic audience, the effort is fruitless. Over the years I have had many examples of this—the most important being Vietnam. On far too many occasions, what we describe as bad or inadequate journalism is actually bad or inadequate education on the part of the journalistic audience.

Even though the coverage of the special session in 1939 did not advance my knowledge of journalism, it did bring me to the realization that there was a fascinating Senate process that was worth making an effort to understand. I did make the effort but the understanding did not come quickly. I was too bound by the conventions of journalism. A war intervened and after the war a couple of years covering the House of Representatives. It was not until 1953 that I found myself in a position where I could really observe the Senate at work from a platform that did not distort the view. It was the Senate Democratic Policy Committee with Lyndon B. Johnson as chairman.

Some words of explanation are necessary in order to put the Policy Committee into focus. It was an outgrowth of the LaFollette-Monroney Legislative Reorganization Act of 1946. This was a measure that was unpopular with most of the members of both the House and the Senate. It carried provisions to consolidate committees, set up a "legislative budget," and provide leadership committees that would state Democratic and Republican "policy" on major issues. These ideas were welcomed by legislators in the same spirit that picnickers would welcome a swarm of mosquitoes. The committee consolidation would eliminate treasured chairmanships; the legislative budget would reduce the room for maneuver on appropriations and the policy committees would inevitably provoke clashes with members who felt that their primary allegiance was to their constituencies rather than to party organization.

The measure was passed only because it included a badly needed pay raise for Senators and Representatives. The merits of the raise—in view of the inflation that had taken place since the last one—were undeniable. But Congressmen are placed in a peculiar trap on such an issue. They are in the unfortunate position of being the only body that can set its own pay rates, and because it must be done with tax money, their constituents are not very sympathetic. Whenever they reach a point where the raise is ready to go through, they start grasping for excuses. In this instance, their claim was that the reorganization act would make them more efficient and therefore they were entitled to more money.

The bill passed but about the only provision that was carried out as advertised was the pay raise. The committees were consolidated but each one promptly set up scores of subcommittees complete with chairman, stationery, and staff. The legislative budget provision was simply ignored for more than thirty years. The House rejected the Policy Committee idea altogether. In the Senate, the Policy Committee was turned into a public relations group for the Republicans and a source of extra staff for the floor leader on the Democratic side of the aisle. At no time did it ever fill the role envisaged by the authors of the bill.

In practice, the Senate Democratic Policy Committee became whatever the floor leader wanted it to be. I was fortunate in that I was made director under Lyndon Johnson. He looked upon it as a device for working out the compromises that were needed to enact legislation and the purpose of the staff was to explore possible compromises. This meant that I and my colleagues were in constant touch with the members of the Senate, exploring their thinking and attempting to devise amendments and strategies for floor debate. There simply could not be a better vantage point. It was, however, very delicate business. The Senate is a body of individualists, and a member who feels that his or her toes are being stepped on has many ways of teaching the offender a lesson.

The substance of any bill that came before us had already been explored by legislative committees and we had to be careful not to duplicate their work. Basically, we approached all measures with two questions in our minds. First, what had to be done to the act, if anything, to secure its passage; second, would the bill, after needed amendments had been made, retain enough merit to justify passage? Obviously, we were proceeding on the "half a loaf of bread is better than no loaf" theory at which many people scoff. But it seems to me that the scoffers must be men and women who have never been hungry.

This is the point at which my education in the Senate began. It was not easy. I had too much intellectual baggage to clear out of my mind before there could be room for reality. Despite years of experience as a legislative reporter, I still clung to concepts that just weren't so. For example, I was under the delusion, cultivated by Wilson, that the committee chairmen were all-powerful tyrants who ran the body in total disregard of the wishes of the rest of its members. I regarded the rules as barriers set up to prevent progress in the area of civil rights—and also thought there *could* be progress if only the rules were changed. Even today, I can blush over the memory of my naïveté.

My real mentor in the Senate, however, was not Johnson but Richard B. Russell of Georgia. He was regarded as The Enemy by most liberals of that period because he was the leader of the Southern bloc, which had successfully bottled up all action on civil rights. That did not prevent

13

the liberals from running to him for shelter, when General Douglas MacArthur returned from Korea.

The recall of MacArthur by President Truman set off one of the great emotional binges of American history. The General had clearly been insubordinate. His so-called plan for ending the war in Korea was shot through with holes. That did not matter. He was a commanding presence, a superb orator, and Americans were sick and-tired of a war that could not be "won." The huge crowds that assembled to see him when he reached Washington, D.C., were in a mood to seize the White House physically and hand it to him. He received an invitation to address a joint session of Congress. His words—topped off with an old, maudlin barracks room ballad, "Old Soldiers Never Die"—raised popular emotions to a fever pitch and it was obvious that they could not be cooled by pretending that nothing had happened. Congress had to do something that would respond either affirmatively or negatively to the widespread belief that a patriot with a program to end a war was being shoved aside by an administration that was incompetent and possibly infested with traitors.

The response of the Senate was to combine the Senate Foreign Relations and the Senate Military Affairs committees into a body of joint inquiry. Russell, who was chairman of the Military Affairs group, was selected to preside. The reason for the choice was obvious. He was regarded as the only member of the Senate with sufficient ability to survive the political hazards inherent in such an undertaking. What was more important to me was that Lyndon Johnson "loaned" me to Russell for the duration of the hearings. It was quite a transition. My last act for the United Press had been to cover MacArthur's entrance

14

into the Hotel Statler when he arrived in Washington. My first act for the Senate—my new employer—was to act unofficially as the staff for the MacArthur hearings.

It was a strange relationship. Russell and I agreed on very little in the political world. But we both had a deep sense of the vital necessity of reestablishing the principle of civilian control over the military. As a result, our relationship became very close. It was a difficult situation, as only Russell, Johnson, and a few of Russell's staff members knew of my role. I would work late into the night analyzing transcripts of testimony and writing memoranda for the chairman. We would have brief conferences in the morning before I went home to get some sleep. Russell's presiding was masterly and served to quiet down the furor. But what also happened is that I became very close to a man who was the preeminent senatorial tactician—a man who understood the workings of that body in depth and who combined his tremendous parliamentary skill with a grasp of history that was equaled by very few politicians in my memory.

I intend to cover the MacArthur hearings at a later point in this book and also to say more about Russell. What is important here is some concept of the world into which I was introduced. Russell may have been the key that opened the doors of my Senate knowledge. The MacArthur hearings had taken place well before I became staff director of the Policy Committee (Johnson originally hired me to write reports for his Preparedness Investigating Subcommittee) but the experience I gained from the hearings paved the way for the committee post. The eight years that followed were the years in which I learned through the hardest but most effective of all schools—the knowledge that arises from day-to-day work with an organization.

The most important lesson I had to learn during those years is that power in the Senate has nothing to do with organizational machinery. Every member has precisely the same power standing as every other member. The House of Representatives is controlled by blocs to which the members are subordinate. Parliaments are controlled by political party machinery, which is run by hierarchies. Blocs exist in the Senate but they are fluid. Senators shift from bloc to bloc according to the issue. Their votes are their own. This does not mean that they all have the same power or the same status. But it does mean that they all have the same *instrument* of power—one vote. The determinant factor is how they use that vote—whether they merely cast it in favor of measures that they support and against measures that they do not support, or whether they also trade their votes for positions of advantage. The life of the Senate is very much like the game of go, in which both players have precisely the same instruments at hand and in which the rules are extraordinarily simple. The play consists of laying down counters alternately until one side has surrounded the other. If one can think of that game as being played with 100 contestants on the same board, one will have a perfect picture of the Senate of the United States.

The reality is obscured by the obviously commanding position of the committee chairmen. There is no question but that they exercise more influence than other members. This has led to the widespread belief that the determining factor in the operation of the Senate is seniority. The reality, however, is that the committee chairmen are usually powerful because they have more political ability than other members. Survival *is* a test of political ability and survivability is essential to seniority. If one looks at the records of the committee chairmen one will usually find that they had gained their Senate powers long before they became chairmen. Furthermore, there are some instances in which incompetent Senators arose to committee chairmanships and the situation caused no problem whatsoever. During the period I was directing the Policy Committee staff, one chairman of a key committee had literally become senile. When we had business involving his committee, Senate protocol required me to pay a courtesy call upon him. It took all of five minutes and would be followed by a direct visit with the fourth ranking committee Democrat, who was actually running the show. At all times, chairmen who were out of step with the majority were easily bypassed but the methods of doing it were so tactful and graceful that it was not apparent to the public.

This point becomes more comprehensible when it is contrasted with the situation in the House of Representatives. In that body, a committee chairman really has power. Should he become senile, the House lacks the graceful machinery of the Senate and can go around him only by awkward and very obvious maneuvering. Should he be out of step with his colleagues, the effort required to get a bill to the floor past his disapproval is so great that it will be attempted only under the most compelling circumstances. One of the heaviest burdens carried by the late Sam Rayburn as Speaker of the House was the iron control exercised over the House Rules Committee by conservative Southern Democrats and Republicans. As all House bills must go through that committee before getting to the floor (there are a few exceptions but they are not worth covering here), its power was tremendous and it was used to frustrate the Speaker on many occasions. The fact that such power cannot be exercised in the Senate speaks volumes about the differences between the two chambers.

The concept of an inner "club" that directs the operations of the Senate is much closer to validity than the seniority theory. However, the terms of admission must be understood. It is not a club composed of like-minded men and women, and admission is open to all who understand it. Some men and women become members the day they walk into the Senate—notably Lyndon B. Johnson, Robert S. Kerr, and Eugene Millikin. Others (for charitable reasons, I will not name them) can serve two or even three terms and never even locate the front door. The club roster included Senators as liberal as Hubert Humphrey and Thomas Kuchel and as conservative as John Stennis and Styles Bridges. And from the list of names I have supplied in this paragraph, it should be obvious that party divisions have nothing to do with the situation. Finally, it should be added that formal positions of status are only indirectly related. Senator William F. Knowland, the Republican leader of the Senate during many of the years I am covering, had a bare toehold on membership. He lacked the natural instincts that make for preeminence in the chamber.

What really holds the members of "the club" together is a mutual recognition that *all* members have constituency pressures that are overriding. This makes for a great deal of back scratching and horse trading. But it also gives a degree of cohesion without which the affairs of the Senate would be very chaotic indeed. At one end of the spectrum, it can produce Senators whose sole purpose in life is to act as errand boy for their constituents. But at the other end, it produces Senators who regard vote trading as one means of building support for causes in which they have deep moral convictions. Hubert Humphrey, for example, used some of his vote swaps to gain support for civil rights legislation from Senators outside the South who otherwise would have given covert aid to the Dixie resistance.

The nonmembers of the club are those who will not—or cannot—recognize the constituency problems of their fellow legislators. Generally speaking, they are the ultraliberals or the ultraconservatives as both groups entertain the curious delusion that they have a monopoly on political morality. When it comes to getting something done in the Senate, they are totally ineffective. But this judgment must be accompanied by another evaluation. It is that without their presence, the Senate would become a stultifying operation. Nothing can be done without the club members. But left to their own devices, there would be very little change no matter how pressing the need for change. The "ultras" keep the pot boiling, and while their simplistic concepts are not as fascinating as the subtleties of the club members, it would be an unhappy day for the country if they were eliminated.

What I hope to do in this book is to provide some insights into the manner in which the Senate worked during the 1950s. Naturally, I am writing about that period because it is one in which my knowledge is firsthand. That alone, however, would not justify this effort either by me or by the publisher. What does justify the effort is that the decade was one in which the Senate really worked. The previous years had been barren and in none of the years that have followed has the body been so productive. Of course, there have been many changes in our society since the fifties. We are a different nation socially, economically, and politically. Many of the achievements of the fifties would not be possible today. But we can still learn from observation of a period in which a political and governmental body did what it was supposed to do.

2

A Body That Does Nothing

For this book to serve any purpose, it is essential to probe more deeply than we have into the causes for the large-scale public misunderstanding of the nature and function of the Senate. There are many reasons, some of which we have covered already. But most of them boil down to the simple fact that the body does not *do* anything, in the sense that most Americans understand the word "do." It does not manufacture gadgets, sweep the streets, enforce laws, make insurance payments, sell stocks and bonds, or defend the nation. In terms of public esteem, this situation places it at a disadvantage when contrasted with private industry or executive agencies of the government, which are "doers" who engage in such enterprises.

The essence of Senate activity is the engineering of a

national consensus. But, as we have already explained, the engineering of consensus is not an activity that is readily comprehensible to most of our people nor is it compatible with the requirements of a system of mass communications. Therefore, Americans tend to concentrate on secondary activities that they can understand—or at least think they can understand. Inevitably, this leads to a situation in which the members who have the least to do with the true functions of the body, or members who add a secondary sideline to their legislative work, command the dominant position in public recognition. They do so either by launching a spectacular investigation of something or by becoming the leaders *outside the Senate* of a burning cause. Either course, incidentally, has a tendency to diminish legislative effectiveness.

It is no accident, in my judgment, that the three Senators who became Presidents during my time in Washington were all involved in investigations that made headlines. John F. Kennedy probed into labor racketeering; Richard M. Nixon will go to his grave best known (aside from Watergate) for his work in the Alger Hiss case; Lyndon B. Johnson entered the ring of serious White House possibilities through his inquiry into outer space. Of the three, only Johnson's investigation made a strong impact upon the legislative process—it led to the passage of the Outer Space Act. The point becomes even clearer when one considers the Senators who were given serious consideration for the job but who did not make the Presidency. They included such men as Estes Kefauver, Richard Russell, and Hubert H. Humphrey. The latter two men possessed a large amount of legislative skill but their public reputations were based upon their role as pro and con symbols of the civil rights debate.

In some respects, Kefauver is the most interesting of them all. There was probably no member of the United States Senate who commanded a more fanatical following in the country during the fifties. Liberals reacted to him in the same mood of ecstasy displayed by teenage groupies during Elvis Presley concerts. They were his—body and soul. Futhermore, his name *was* a household word. Even those who hated him knew who he was. Part of this was due to his appearance. He was tall, ugly in a Lincolnesque sort of way, awkward in carriage, and possessed with a slow drawl that somehow converted the most banal phrases into deeply moving messages (I never discovered the nature of the messages but his followers assured me they were profound).

The Kefauver standing in the Senate was something else. He had irritated all of the powerhouses by his adamant refusal to recognize that his colleagues might have problems. He had a simple formula for determining his stance on any legislative issue. If a social program was before the Senate—housing, education, medical care, slum clearance, or anything else in that category—he would move to double it. It didn't matter whether money was available, needed, or even spendable (in medical research, for example, money cannot always be spent because of a lack of researchers). He could be relied upon to come through with an amendment. This meant that many of his colleagues were put upon a spot. To support his amendments was irresponsibility. To oppose his amendments was to alienate some constituents. He rarely succeeded in getting roll call votes that would have put the members squarely on the record. But that did not prevent embarrassing questions. Had he limited his tactic to a few choice items that were politically important to him, he would have been forgiven. He pushed it beyond tolerable limits and became so isolated from mainstream Senate activity that his colleagues winced every time he announced his support of their measures. His approval could be the kiss of death.

His impotence in the arena of legislative action, however, was accompanied by positive brilliance in the arena of public attention. His campaign for the Senate had required him to defeat the hand-picked candidate of one of the last truly powerful city bosses—Ed Crump of Memphis, Tennessee. Crump, at one point, referred to Kefauver as a "pet coon"—the biggest mistake Crump ever made. Kefauver promptly donned a coonskin cap and announced that he might be a "pet coon" but he wasn't "Ed Crump's pet coon." He then made Crump *the* campaign issue and persuaded the voters that it was a contest between an honest, clean man of the people and a wily, corrupt political manipulator. When the smoke of battle finally cleared, Ed Crump could be described only in the past tense; Estes Kefauver had become the shining knight who had killed the dragon; and the coonskin cap had become a nationwide symbol for Estes and purity. It was breathtaking.

At best, his career in the Senate could be described as "routine" in terms of legislative achievement. No important law emerged with his name on it; he sparked no Congressional strategy that changed the philosophy or the general direction of the government; he was not even as good as his predecessors (who had been Ed Crump men body and soul) in bringing choice federal morsels back to his native Tennessee. But when he succeeded in gaining the chairmanship of a committee investigation of organized crime in the United States, he became, virtually overnight, the most widely known member of the United States Senate.

The investigation was a dramatic presentation. Television was still young but out of its infancy and Estes Kefauver was one of the first politicians to recognize its potential. His committee provided a backdrop for a parade of sleazy characters before the camera lens and it was quickly recognized as one of the best—if not the best—TV dramas in America. The show had everything. There were menacing hoodlums who acted as the "heavies." There were tales of interstate plots to subvert governments and control all types of illegal traffic. There was even comic relief in the form of gamblers with Runyonesque names and vocabularies. The high point came with the questioning of Frank Costello, whom many believed to be the summit of organized crime in America. Costello objected to being televised and an agreement was reached that the cameras would not pick up his face while he was on the witness stand. Instead, they focused on his hands, providing one of the most fascinating visual effects in the entire history of the electronic medium. Costello's fingers went through a continuing pattern of drumming, interlacing, pointing, arching, and expressing emotions much more clearly than his face itself. For those who saw it, the session was unforgettable.

No one can make a convincing case that the Kefauver hearings put any serious crimp in the operations of organized crime in America. But the evidence is incontrovertible that Kefauver himself emerged from the experience as the Democratic leader with the most enthusiastic following in the United States. The age of the political boss was drawing rapidly to a close. It was the dawn of mass communication politics in which electoral success depended upon a politician's ability to move large numbers of people who were paying more attention to the words spoken on their TV than to the words spoken by their precinct captains. Tammany and men such as Hague, Kelly, Arvey, and Crump were becoming liabilities rather than assets. Except for Richard Daley in Chicago, they could no longer deliver votes and they had no television presence whatsoever. Their names smacked of boodlery, sleaze, and cynicism—qualities that always provoke opposition when they are unaccompanied by the general dispensation of largesse that was possible in the heyday of the big-city machine.

The demise of bossdom was much more critical for Democrats than for Republicans. Both parties had rested upon machines. But the city organizations had been largely Democratic—simply because they were based upon immigrants from Ireland and eastern and southern Europe, who tended to settle in urban areas. The GOP organizations usually centered around statehouses and their troops were composed of WASPs and immigrants from northern Europe who were less susceptible to the adversary criticism of political reformers. They were not as blatant, and their operations were scattered over large areas where it was difficult to pin down any hanky-panky at the polls. City leaders were obvious in their machinations. Not only were they unsubtle men but they lived in an environment that militated against subtlety.

The importance of the city machines to the Democratic Party was underlined by the refusal of Democratic Presidents to move against them even as late as Harry S Truman. Franklin Delano Roosevelt never laid a glove on Ed Kelly, Boss Hague, or Dave Lawrence. Truman did his best to rescue Pendergast from jail and even Jack Kennedy acknowledged to friends the debt that he owed to Richard Daley. But the victory of Dwight D. Eisenhower in 1952 persuaded many Democrats that they had to disassociate themselves from machine politics. To them, Kefauver was a godsend—the champion of the people who had bested in honorable combat organized crime with which urban political organizations—whether fairly or unfairly—were tied in the public mind. "Estes is the bestest" became the slogan of the liberals in the Democratic Party who had always had some reservations about the ties to the seamier city wards.

Twice Kefauver mounted major drives for the Democratic Presidential nomination. The first time, he lost out to a combination of anti–civil rights Southern Democrats and city bosses, most of whom could no longer deliver votes in a general election but who could control the selection of state delegations. The second time, he ran against a man who for a variety of reasons was unbeatable—Adlai Stevenson. As soon as Stevenson was nominated, however, he announced that he would allow the convention to select the Vice Presidential nominee. Kefauver won easily, forging ahead of John F. Kennedy in the process. After the defeat of the Democratic ticket, the magic faded quickly and it is doubtful whether his name would be widely recognized today even in his native Tennessee. But to students of the history of the United States Senate he remains as one of the best examples of how far a member can go in terms of public recognition without participating in any of the body's fundamental activities.

Jack Kennedy, of course, went even further in that he succeeded in snaring not only the Presidential nomination but the Presidency itself. The story, however, is not quite as dramatic. Behind Kennedy were fantastic resources that were never under Kefauver's command. Through his family, Kennedy had access to money and to organizational resources that no other politician could match. Furthermore, he was young, vibrant, and available at just about the time that the World War II generation decided to take over the direction of the nation. His legislative achievements, aside from the labor racketeering investigation, were practically nil but his position in the Senate gave him a sounding board. He did not engender the enmity of his Senate colleagues, as did Kefauver, simply because he did not interfere with them. One had the feeling that the Capitol Building was a *pied-à-terre* that he also used as a mailing address in Washington, D.C.

The senior members of the Senate regarded Kennedy as something of a lightweight. His only impact upon legislation was that of a single vote. Sometimes even that was not available, as he avoided most controversies. He had written a book entitled *Profiles in Courage,* which told the tales of Senators who had exhibited unusual degrees of bravery in casting unpopular votes. On one occasion, when Kennedy had managed to avoid a really "hot potato" type of decision, Senator George Smathers of Florida, a close friend, said to him: "Jack, I sure would like to see more courage and less profile." This attitude was not conveyed to the public. The Senate itself does not issue report cards on the conduct of its members and the ratings lists issued every year by such groups as Americans for Democratic Action or Americans for Conservative Action reveal nothing except attitudes.

This attitude did not bother Kennedy in the slightest. Like his younger brother Robert, he was an "action" man who could not work up any interest in the subtleties of engineering consensus in the Senate. (In fairness, it should be added that his youngest brother—Ted—*does* have the legislative temperament and is a major figure in the upper chamber of Congress. This may be one of the reasons why his Presidential bids have failed.) He began drawing a bead on the Presidency as early as 1956 and by 1960 a formidable organization was in place. It was not, however, an organization that exuded an aura of the city machine. Jack Kennedy was descended from a famous machine man—John J. "Honey Fitz" Fitzgerald. But he had learned to recruit the intellectuals and whenever one looked at his followers, the men up front were Ivy League academic—Schlesinger, Galbraith, Wofford et al. It may well have been that the levers of real power were being exercised by men such as O'Brien and O'Donnell but they were keeping out of sight.

Richard M. Nixon was another illustration of the possibilities open to a member of Congress who really does not care about its activities. There was never a moment in his legislative career that he was considered a serious factor in shaping the laws of the land. But he did have an eye on the opportunities available in both the House and the Senate for a man who wishes to capture the public imagination. I can best illustrate the point by a personal story.

At the end of World War II when I returned to Washington from the Army Air Force, I was assigned by the United Press to cover the House of Representatives. During the years 1947 and 1948 that turned out to be an assignment that left me covering two stories, virtually full time. One was the passage of the Taft-Hartley labor law.

The other was the Congressional investigation of Alger Hiss and other alleged communist spies. Nixon was a member of both committees involved. During the entire course of consideration of the Taft-Hartley Act, I doubt whether I checked with Nixon more than two or three times because I discovered early that he had neither information nor views worth taking up my time. On one occasion he expressed to me some dubiety about the secondary boycott features of the act and predicted there would be a "young Turk" revolt against the Republican leadership. Within hours after the story appeared in print, he repudiated it. On legislation, he was strictly a follower unable to stand against the top GOP members. On the Alger Hiss case, however, he turned out to be the only reliable source of information. Of course, he did not tell us all he knew and we (the press) were sufficiently suspicious to check out all of his facts. But he was obviously the driving force behind the inquiry and the facts he gave us were always facts—which could not be said of any other committee member. The point was clear. In the investigative realm under the light of publicity, he was a dominant figure. In the legislative realm, he stood in the shadows.

The Hiss investigation was sufficient to propel him into the Senate. From there, by astute maneuvering at the Republican convention, he snagged the Vice Presidential nomination to run with Dwight D. Eisenhower—the most unbeatable White House candidate of the century. When he was defeated in 1960 running for the top job in his own right, he began an assiduous courtship of the powers-that-be in the GOP, which paid off in his election as Chief Executive in 1968. To those who remembered him from the legislative days, it was hard to think of him as a political power. Actually, he was an effective President who may well be treated in good grace by history regardless of the horrors of Watergate. He may have lacked the legislative temperament but he understood the usages of Executive power.

In terms of legislative achievement, it would be impossible to find a national leader of greater stature than Richard B. Russell of Georgia. With Russell's blessing, almost any measure could pass the Senate. Against his determined opposition, it was doomed. He was not only subtle, he had a grasp of history with a long view of both the past and the future. Above all, he was clear-eyed. More than any other man I have ever met, he could see what was there to see, even when he didn't like it. He was recognized on both sides of the aisle as the preeminent Senator—so much so that it was almost automatic for the Senate to put him in charge of the potentially explosive inquiry into the return of General MacArthur from Korea. It is doubtful whether any other member could have succeeded in defusing the bomb.

To the nation at large, however, he was known only as the symbol of resistance to the civil rights movement. His legislative skill did absolutely nothing to offset the Northern picture of Russell as Simon Legree driving the black slaves to work with a whip early in the morning. Consequently, when he announced his candidacy for the Presidency in 1952, it was assumed that this was the Confederate bid to crush civil rights within the Democratic Party.

The reality was more complicated. Actually, his Presidential bid began in his office in a conference with me and Lyndon Johnson. It was based on a plan to head off the danger that the Southern delegates to the Democratic Convention would walk out and join the Eisenhower crusade in protest against the inevitable Democratic endorsement of civil rights.

The idea worked according to the plan, which will be described later. The South did stay within the Democratic Party formally, even though many of its voters went for Eisenhower. It was also, however, a moment of high tragedy. One of the ablest minds American politics has ever produced could get consideration for the top spot through a political ploy that had only indirect relevancy to a genuine campaign.

Hubert H. Humphrey was another example of a man who had a high degree of legislative ability but who came close to the Presidency only because he was a cause leader outside the Senate. He was a man of great appeal—brimming with energy; bubbling over with a youthful optimism that did not desert him right up to his dying day; and so articulate that the problem was to persuade him to stop—rather than start—talking. Above all, he could "swing" with an audience. To attend a Hubert Humphrey "speaking" was to sense the same emotions that Baptist preachers and rock 'n' roll bands bring into play. To all that should be added the fact that he was a very serious politician who wanted to get things done. The phrase "the happy warrior of the political battlefields" applied to him even more than it did to Al Smith but it must be realized that there was an equal accent on the two words "happy" and "warrior."

Humphrey had both the capacity and the temperament to deal with the legislative problems of forging a consensus. However, all his previous experience had been on the executive side of government, either as a state administrator of the National Youth Administration or mayor of Minneapolis. He had spent his adult life negotiating work projects for young people; inspecting a city police force and keeping it up to the mark; making sure that garbage was collected on time; finding housing and food for homeless people. The Senate environment was baffling to him. In the terms of his past existence, he had nothing to do. A Senator's staff is small and runs itself; perhaps the Senator is allotted a patronage policeman but that is not quite the same thing as operating a whole force; the collection of garbage is the responsibility of the housekeeping staff. There had to be some outlet for the supercharged Humphrey energy and he finally came to the conclusion that Senators make speeches. He plunged right in.

Within a week, Humphrey had qualified for the title SMUB—The Senate's Most Unmitigated Bore. No session could go by without a lengthy disquisition on civil rights. Had the topic varied, it might have been endurable. Had there been a legislative point to his remarks, members would have groaned inwardly but kept quiet and remained ready to do business with him when he was so inclined. In the Senate of the United States, hot air is forgivable when it serves a purpose even when the members are not in sympathy with that purpose. But when words are intended only to educate people in a cause, the speaker is soon frozen out of the life of the chamber. Senators do not regard themselves as forming an educational institution.

Lyndon Johnson finally came to Hubert's rescue. It happened one morning shortly before a Senate session. Johnson and I were just preparing to board the subway train that takes Senators and staff members from the Senate Office Building to the Capitol when Humphrey emerged from another door on the same errand. I quickly shifted my seat so the two could sit together, but the cars were so small that I could hear the conversation clearly. LBJ opened in what was virtually a worshipful tone of voice.

"Hubert," he said. "You have no idea what a wonderful experience it is for me to ride to the Senate chamber with you in the morning. There are so many ways that I envy you. You are articulate; you have such a vast field of knowledge; you have command of such a huge flow of words; you can speak with such absolute logic."

LBJ paused to let his words sink in. Humphrey was almost purring like a kitten before a warm bowl of milk. Then the boom was lowered.

"But God damn it, Hubert," Johnson barked in a sudden change of voice. "Why can't you be something but a gramophone for the NAACP? God damn it, Hubert, why can't you make a speech about labor for once? God damn it, Hubert, why can't you make a speech about farmers? God damn it, Hubert, why can't you make a speech to help the old folks? God damn it, Hubert, why can't you make a speech about education for poor people? And God damn it, Hubert, why can't you do something for all those people *and* the NAACP besides talking about them. You're spending so much time making speeches that there is no time left to get anything done."

The lesson struck home. To everybody's relief, Hubert became quiet and started to work on bills. The speeches in the Senate were reserved for legislation before the Senate, and within a year or two, he was definitely a member of "the club." The "liberal bloc" negotiated through him during the crucial maneuvers that led to passage of the Civil Rights Act of 1957—the first to get through the Senate since 1875. Had the liberal bloc been represented by a less able negotiator, there would have been no bill. However, he did *not* drop his speechifying altogether. He merely moved it to areas outside the Senate. He had the knack of hanging on to leadership of the cause in the public arena and without that knack he would not have become Vice President of the United States and a Democratic candidate who missed the Presidency by one of the narrowest margins in history.

There was, of course, one man who was in perfect tune with the United States Senate and who still made the Presidency. That was Lyndon Baines Johnson. He was universally acknowledged as one of the ablest legislative leaders in history; and for part of his Presidential administration he was one of the more popular Presidents in history. When one traces his path to the White House, however, it becomes apparent that he was no exception to the general rule. He merely happened to be standing in the right place at the right time and his superb legislative record was a stumbling block rather than an asset on his journey to the American political summit. To the public at large, his operations in the Senate smacked too much of "log rolling," "wheeling and dealing," "horse trading," and all the other pejorative phrases we apply to the workings of democracy.

Johnson himself ascribed his inability to mount an effective Presidential campaign to his Southern origins. This never made much sense to me. Kefauver represented an ex-Confederate state and the fact never hurt his Presidential ambitions. Furthermore, as a certified Northerner, I was aware of the fact that Northerners think of Texas in terms of cowboys and chuck wagons rather than cotton and slaves. Furthermore, he had been the driving force that rammed through the Senate the Civil Rights Act of 1957. It turned out that this feat—which was little short of a miracle—served only to take him out of the Northern category of extreme bigot. It was assumed that as leader of the Senate he could have passed a much stronger bill had he so wished. I discovered that for non-senatorial types, it was impossible to refute this argument effectively. They knew so little about legislative procedure that they could not appreciate the fantastic amount of effort that had been required.

What launched him on the path to the Presidency was the inquiry into the outer space effort that followed the orbiting of the Soviet satellite Sputnik. Here was something that people could understand—or at least thought they could understand. Witnesses were selected with care for their dramatic value. The hearings opened with the physicist Edward Teller, who could give a portentous reading of the New York City telephone book and convince his listeners that it was a prophecy of doom. A picture built up rapidly of a universe in which the Soviet Union was well on its way to control of the space around the earth and thus to assert mastery over everything on our planet. The Eisenhower administration made the mistake of downplaying the importance of the hearings—elevating Johnson himself to the level of the Presidency. He appeared as the last-ditch defense against invaders from outer space.

In retrospect, the hearings were definitely overdrawn.

They produced, for example, the famous "missile gap," which never actually existed but which did lead many Americans to believe that the Soviets had overwhelming might at their command and that we were virtually helpless to fight back in case of an attack. (It should be added that the gap, which was featured by John F. Kennedy in the 1960 Presidential campaign, was a good faith interpretation of the figures. In the cold afterlight, it also turned out to be an unjustified interpretation made by men who were overly eager to find it.) At the same time, however, it definitely placed Lyndon B. Johnson into the class where he could be considered for the Presidency. At the 1960 Democratic convention, he offered the only significant opposition to Kennedy and his selection as the Vice Presidential candidate unified the party for the campaign.

The point still remains that among the abler legislators, there are very few who can count on entering the White House in any capacity other than guest. Those few will be men (and women) who have ignored or soft-pedaled legislative work and have concentrated on investigations or leadership—*outside* the Senate—of public causes. It is unfortunate that Congress is not better understood. We pass up some real talent because of our ignorance.

3
The Fine Art of Voting

Before going too deeply into the history of the Senate during the 1950s, it would be well to delve into the fine art of voting. To the public at large—and to many Senators who never master the realities of the body—a vote is simply a determinant to an issue. It is cast to support, oppose, or modify. The entrance to "the club" comes only when the member discovers the subtleties that are associated with the deceptively simple act of saying "yea" or "nay." To the initiate, the problem of voting must be considered not only in terms of the merits of the issue but also in terms of its relationship to the past and the future. There are three fundamental considerations:

First, every vote becomes part of a long-range record that will be scrutinized by both friend and foe at the next election.

Second, every vote is conditioned to some extent by past votes and, in turn, sets up conditions for the next vote. (A good parallel is the strategy of a billiards player who not only sinks a ball with each shot but sets up the cue ball so he can make the next shot.)

Third, the vote can be used to pay off obligations to other Senators or place other Senators under obligations to be paid off at some future date. It is trading currency as well as an instrument of power.

These considerations impart to the Senators who have mastered them a strong sense of continuity. In their minds, no vote is ever final. It is merely one battle in a continuing set of engagements that never really come to an end. The specifics of an issue may disappear but they will be replaced by new specifics that will be fought out on the same battlefields. For this reason, the effective Senators do not regard compromise as immoral per se, even though they may have strong moral standards to apply to the issues themselves. Here, they contrast strongly with Senators outside "the club." The latter tend to regard every legislative clash as Armageddon and every compromise as a deal with the devil. Their votes are predictable and consequently they have very little trading power.

The sanctity of voting is guarded jealously by the Senate. It takes very seriously the provision of the Constitution that says that no state may be deprived of equal representation in the Senate under any circumstances. This is why Vice Presidents are always treated so coldly by the body. They are suspected of trying to insert an extra vote into the works—a thought that is absolutely intolerable to the members. Lyndon Johnson discovered in 1961 that his position as Vice President virtually isolated him from any real life in the Senate. He attempted to attend Democratic caucuses and was ejected politely, but firmly, on the grounds that he was now a member of the executive branch of the government. Under the Constitution, the Vice President is supposed to preside over the Senate. He rarely does. I suspect that this is because he does not like to spend the day facing the wave of hostility, which is very thinly concealed. Theoretically, his presence is needed to break tie votes. But on most tie votes his side wins anyway. There are never more than two or three a year where he can make a real difference.

The vote, of course, is usually the culmination of long periods of negotiation. The basic work of the Senate is done neither in committee nor on the floor, although both places play important roles in the process. The committees gather the facts at leisure, which means that when they finish with a bill, its provisions are thoroughly understood. The floor debate builds a record for the courts and for the executive branch of the government on legislative intent and also legitimizes an act. But the actual shaping of a measure is the result of thousands of hours of quiet conversation—of talks while walking down a corridor; or over cups of coffee; or at parties; or in the cloak rooms. The real reason visitors so rarely see the Senate filled with members is that most of them are out engaging in these chats. The true life of the Senate is out of sight of the spectators.

It would be a mistake to assume that these conversations and negotiations are merely horse trading. They are also a means of taking soundings to measure the depth of the opposition and to find vulnerable spots into which amendments can be slipped and the whole course of the debate altered. The conversation is incessant, so much so that often Senators reveal important information without realizing themselves that they are doing it. For example, the jury trial amendment that made possible the passage of the Civil Rights Act of 1957 was drawn up because continual negotiations with the Southerners had made it clear that this really was a sticking point. They did not dare go home with a law that carried with it criminal penalties to be assessed without a jury trial. But they never asked for an amendment because they assumed it would not be forthcoming.

During my college days, I was taught that a model economic absurdity would be a community where everyone lived by taking in each other's washing. In a sense, the Senate is like that—a community where everyone lives by taking in each other's intellectual washing. It should be added that the process involves not only Senators but staff members. They, too, spend their days talking to each other, and the information they exchange eventually gets into the hands of their principals. Bobby Baker, the Secretary of the Majority, built quite an empire for himself because he was so adept at picking the right senatorial ears into which to pour what he had picked up in the course of his daily rounds. Johnson relied on him heavily for advance warning on Senators who were straying off the reservation.

An understanding of this process is the key to understanding power in the Senate. There is no position that in and of itself carries grants of authority. At one point, I searched the records, the precedents, and the memories of old-timers to determine just what control, if any, was possessed by the floor leader. The only thing I could find was a well-recognized custom that the floor leaders would get priority in recognition when they sought it from the floor. However, the fact that there was no position of authority did not mean that there was no power. Those Senators who knew how to handle themselves in the maneuvering that went on every day could take almost any position and convert it into power.

An outstanding example was Senator Carl Hayden of Arizona, chairman of the Senate Rules Committee and a leading member (and later chairman) of the Senate Appropriations Committee. Obviously, his place on the Appropriations Committee placed him at a key money point, and he used it for all it was worth. But he also learned how to convert the Senate Rules Committee—normally an innocuous group—into a power base. He did so by astute use of its housekeeping functions. It controlled office assignments, printing, and furniture. That meant that a Senator who wanted to change his office, get a committee report printed, or acquire some new furniture went through Hayden. In addition, Hayden became chairman of the Democratic Patronage Committee, which meant that if the Senator needed to appoint a constituent's son to the job of page boy or Capitol policeman, again he saw Hayden.

What is intersting about this situation is that it constituted power that did not belong to previous or succeeding committee chairmen. The composition of the Senate is such that anyone can be bypassed who has not exercised his functions astutely. Under other Senators, the housekeeping functions became purely housekeeping, nothing else.

Another example was the Senate Judiciary Committee, which normally is rather quiet. Under Senator Pat

McCarran of Nevada it became immensely powerful simply because McCarran was a powerful man. The list could be multiplied to great length. Under no circumstances, however, will any Senate position be found that carries the type of weight that goes with posts in the House of Representatives.

The basic reason for this situation is that Representatives spend most of their official lives within the confines of their one committee. To Senators, however, the committee is only a part of their stewardship. They have a tendency to think of themselves as members of the whole body and do not approach any issues with diffidence. This is reflected in the Senate rules.

The rules of the House of Representatives are very complex and it requires months of study to master them. In addition, the seeker after parliamentary skill discovers that he or she must also plow through several shelves full of books entitled *Cannon's Precedents in the House of Representatives*. It is a lot of work but the work is richly rewarding. At the end, the student will have a valid concept of how the House works. The Senate rules, on the other hand, can be mastered by any reasonably intelligent person in the course of an afternoon. That work is *not* richly rewarding, as it will give the reader no sense whatsoever of the workings of the upper chamber. The Senate rules are simply a matter of convenience.

This was another hard lesson for me to understand. When I first came to Washington, I was under the illusion that the Senate rules stood in the way of progress and that the kind of legislation passed by the Senate would change if only the rules were changed. It took me a long time to discover that the Senate only reacts in accord with its power base. This was made clear in 1912 when the Constitution was changed to provide for the direct election of Senators. Prior to that time, the members had been sent to Washington by the state legislatures.

The Senate before the change was quite a different body. For one thing, the members were accountable to the state legislatures, which were controllable bodies. This means that a recalcitrant Senator could have quite a bit of "heat" put upon him provided that the Senate leaders applying the heat were members of the political party that controlled the legislature. During that period, the Senate party caucuses exercised tremendous power. A leader could call a caucus and, if he could get better than a fifty percent vote out of it, all of the members of the caucus were bound. (There were certain exceptions but they are irrelevant for the point being made here.)

This situation may have given President Woodrow Wilson a false sense of security during his first term. The direct election amendment had been approved in 1912 but the class of Senators sent to the Senate that year were still provided by the state legislatures. Therefore, when Wilson during his first two years sent proposals to the Congress, the Senate leadership would call a caucus and muster the strength to pass them. In 1915, however, the first class of directly elected Senators entered the chamber and the mood began to change at once. These men felt accountable to the people of their states rather than to their legislatures. To them, the caucus system was a hair shirt. In 1917, the election of another class of Senators raised the number selected by the people to two-thirds of the whole chamber and the caucuses were openly defied. Since that time, there has been no formal machinery controlling the Senate.

This does not mean there are no forms of control. The Senate has ways of disciplining members who offer no co-operation whatsoever to their colleagues. These methods, however, can only be understood in terms of the realities of Senate debate.

As a rule, controversial issues divide the Senate into three major blocs, or groupings, that can be looked upon as a spectrum. At one end, there is a group adamantly opposed to the measure that will bend every effort to seek its defeat. At the other end, there is a group that wants the bill passed exactly as it is and will bend every effort to defeat any modifications. In the middle, there is a key group that ultimately will determine the outcome. Some of its members will be against the bill and some for it but they are held together by a willingness to talk changes and even modify their positions if they can be offered sufficient inducements. Without this middle group, no controversial debate could ever be brought to a conclusion. A leader who really wants to dispose of a divisive issue must create such a moderate center if it does not exist already.

The real legislative process takes place in the middle, where the negotiations eventually bring about a consensus. These are the effective people because they have some elbowroom to do what is necessary. The people at the ends of the spectrum have little to do with the process and usually wind up together voting against the final bill—the supporters because it does not go far enough and the opponents because it goes too far.

What complicates this process is the fact that the Senators rarely wind up in the same group on each debate. The composition of the blocs is constantly shifting. Every Senator at one time or another winds up among the "bitter enders." Even so determined a centrist as Lyndon B.

Johnson had to join extremists on the tidelands issue and the natural gas bill. This is well understood because it results from constituent pressures that everyone feels. A Senator who bobs up too frequently on the ends of the spectrum, however, is a Senator who arouses suspicions in the breasts of his colleagues. They are afraid that this is a man who will not "play the game." Over a period of time, he becomes excluded from the Senate dialogue, which means that he becomes an ineffective Senator. The reason Estes Kefauver incurred the enmity of his colleagues had nothing to do with his liberal stands. Basically, it was because he would not join the centrists at any point. In his case it did not matter because he was shooting for the White House and was indifferent to the maneuverings of his colleagues. To others, however, effectiveness in the Senate was the core of their lives and they would not risk their membership in "the club." To understand this is to understand why the Southerners in 1957 allowed the civil rights bill to go through without a filibuster.

Obviously, true leadership in a body of this character is the exercise of brokerage. In this book we will try to give some idea of what happens when master brokers are in charge.

4

Prelude of Frustration

There is generally an agreement that the Senate from 1952 until 1960 was a highly effective body presided over by a legislative genius—Lyndon B. Johnson. This judgment has a high degree of plausibility and can be defended with very little effort. Unfortunately, it also has a tendency to foster a type of thinking that holds that the problems of attaining meaningful productivity from a legislative body are solely problems of leadership. So many people have said to me—perhaps in the belief that it is a subtle form of flattery—"If only we could get a leader like LBJ, then we could get something done."

In my mind, it does not detract from Lyndon Johnson's high level of parliamentary skill to say that this is nonsense. The operation he maintained during the years from 1952 until 1960 would fail completely today. What is even more important, it would also have failed had he assumed the leadership at any point in the four years that preceded his assumption of the post. His success was basically a matter of a temperament that harmonized precisely with the political conditions that prevailed when Dwight D. Eisenhower took the oath of office as President of the United States. That act changed the whole array of political forces in the nation and made possible an era of productivity in legislation—not because Eisenhower wanted such productivity but because it brought an end to the deep divisiveness that had ruled the nation.

At this point, it is worthwhile to go back and take a look at the conditions that prevailed during the period from 1948 to 1952. From the standpoint of the national government, they were years of discouraging stalemate. Absolutely nothing constructive was done on such pressing issues as civil rights; the condition of agriculture; conservation of natural resources, and sensible development of atomic energy. Most of the time was spent chasing either communist phantoms or communists who had already been exposed as such. Finally, the Korean War blotted everything else off the national agenda.

The conditions of stalemate had appeared even before the election of 1948. Everyone expected Thomas E. Dewey to win and no one was willing to go to bat for President Harry S Truman, who was generally regarded as a lame duck. His unexpected victory in November was dramatic. Not only did he win against all the predictions of the pollsters and the political experts, but he succeeded in bringing in with him a totally Democratic Congress. For a brief period, things looked very bright for the Democrats. The period did not last very long.

First, it turned out that many of the members of the

House and Senate Democratic majorities were of the opinion that they had brought Truman in, rather than the other way around. Second, Truman's persistence on such issues as civil rights did not sit well with Southern Democrats. Third, despite his many years in the Senate Truman had very little skill in dealing with legislative bodies. He was abrasive, contentious, and far too addicted to sending Congress long "laundry lists" of unpassable proposals. The result was the strengthening of the Republican–Southern Democratic coalition.

The Republican–Southern Democratic coalition was an unnatural alliance that existed only because the Southerners were prisoners of the race issue. They had been backed into a corner where they had to pay any price to prevent the passage of civil rights legislation. It was an intolerable situation in the forties and the early fifties because there were still strong currents of populism in Dixie with which many of the Senators were sympathetic. These had to be ignored, as the only way that the drive for legislation to raise the status of racial minorities could be halted was through the cooperation of the Republicans. Unfortunately, the GOP variety of populism, which had once produced effective Senators from the prairie states, was on the wane.

This was a situation in which the Republicans held all the cards. They could go either way on civil rights because they represented constituencies in which it was a secondary (or even tertiary) issue. In addition, they were in a position where they could still pay lip service to racial equality, as the game was to prevent legislation from coming to the floor—not to defeat it once it came before the Senate. In short, they could carry out their end of the bargain with the Southerners without having to go on record. To sweeten the deal, it was apparent that they could walk out of the alliance without suffering any major political damage. To them, the arrangement was a convenience; to the men from south of the Mason-Dixon line, it was an absolute necessity.

The Southerners chafed but could do nothing but grumble among themselves. A few of them (not many) were "pro-labor" but had to go along with the conservatives; many of them were really for rural electrification plans, which had to be sacrificed; many of them favored farm legislation, which went down the drain. After decades of "niggering it" in the South, the politicians of the region were hopelessly trapped. In private conversations, a few were quite frank about their desire for the passage of civil rights legislation to get the monkey off their backs. Unfortunately, they had to oppose it and they had already demonstrated their skill in blocking such laws. Token opposition would not be enough. Of almost equal importance was the fact that the signing of such a bill by a *Democratic* president would create chaos in the political machines of the Southern states. They could not take the risk.

Circumstances had conspired to place them in a situation in which they had no choice. The coalition had to be maintained. For the nation as a whole, however, the coalition had another aspect. It was one that could block legislation but not pass it. What this meant was that nothing happened on the domestic front for four years. The Senate lacked any sense of direction and the leaders were absolutely powerless to do anything other than routine scheduling of appropriation bills. The two men who were

Democratic floor leaders during that period were both retired from office by their constituencies after political careers that had been successful up to the point where they assumed the office.

The only area in which any type of achievement was possible was that of foreign policy legislation. There were two reasons for the exception. The first was that both the Southern Democrats and the Republicans of the Eastern Seaboard had a tendency to be internationally minded. The second was that the main thrust of American foreign policy in that era was anti-Soviet, which meant that it accorded with the anti-communist sentiments boiling so fiercely in the nation. There was strong isolationist sentiment—of the pre–World War II variety—among the Republicans but it could not be said fairly that the party itself was isolationist. Generally speaking, politicians of every stripe were convinced that the United States had to take extraordinary steps to prevent the spread of communism in the world and that meant shoring up allies who were having troubles.

There were, of course, arguments over who should be counted among the allies. The Nationalist regime of Chiang Kai-shek had very strong support in the United States, including people who thought that he had lost mainland China to the communists because of communist sympathizers in the State Department. What was known as "the China lobby" emerged as a major force on the political scene. It was not truly a lobby in the ordinary sense of the word. It included liberals and conservatives, Democrats and Republicans, internationalists and men and women who had previously called themselves isolationists. Some believed in the "treason in the State Department" theory, while others merely thought that the department was wrong in writing off Chiang. It was not a well-organized group. But it had an issue that served as a catalyst for the professional anti-communists who used it to create a turmoil that today seems incredible. It also had a publisher—Henry Luce, of *Time, Life,* and *Fortune*—whose influence upon the political life of the 1950s was awesome.

At this point it is necessary to consider the panic over communism that swept the United States in the years from 1948 to 1952. It was a rather strange phenomenon in that it arose when the Communist Party of the United States was observably on the decline from the positions of power it had once enjoyed. As a political force, it had reached its high-water mark in 1948 in the campaign of the Progressive Party. From there on out, it was all downhill. But as its strength diminished, the concern about it increased to the point of hysteria. This was the era that produced Joe McCarthy and propelled Richard M. Nixon into big-time national politics. (Again, in fairness, it should be stated that Nixon actually had been instrumental in exposing some real communists, including Alger Hiss. McCarthy never proved a single case.) No political leader could plan any move without giving due consideration to the so-called anti-communists whether he was seeking to gain their support or neutralize them. They were such an important factor in public life that at one point Hubert H. Humphrey was actually goaded into sponsorship of a bill to outlaw the Communist Party. He very quickly regretted this move. His liberal friends accused him of turning his back on a lifetime of liberal causes; his conservative enemies gloated over his "capitulation" to them. The measure, which was almost certainly unconstitutional, was lost in a committee pigeonhole.

The China issue was made to order for the times. The American people had been shocked by the revelation that communists had been placed in relatively high positions in the government. But the early exposés did not make it clear that they had done anything that really injured the United States. The mood changed when stories began to appear detailing successful communist espionage attempts during World War II. And when those stories were supplemented by others charging that mainland China had fallen into communist hands because of State Department treachery, a focus was provided to create a major political force. True, the evidence was confusing and disputable but that did not matter. The unarguable fact was that China, the largest nation in the world, had fallen into communist hands and someone was to blame. A few voices were raised on the point that Chiang had simply been incapable of running the nation. But not much attention was paid to them.

There were many reasons for China becoming a central issue in American politics. For one thing, the situation in China was so far outside the ken of the average American that the debate reduced itself to incredible simplicities. Many of our citizens suffered under the delusion that they "knew" about China because they had contributed money every week as a child to some missionary in that country. That—and an occasional dish of chop suey or chow mein—was about their only contact, but it was enough to give them a feeling of familiarity. What may have been even more important is that for obvious reasons the United States treated Chiang Kai-shek during World War II as the head of a united nation. The reality—that he had only nominal authority over a collection of independent warlords—was obscured. Consequently, the communist takeover had the appearance of the overthrow of a giant. This was so far from reality that there was no difficulty in devising and selling myths about what had really happened.

This was a period in which Americans had a tendency to be suspicious of treachery. Very few of our people had enough knowledge of physics to regard the atomic bomb as anything other than a "magic" discovery dependent upon secret formulae. Therefore, when they learned that communist spies had been at work in the atomic energy project, they leaped to the conclusion that their lives had been placed in danger by irresponsible traitors. It took very little for them to connect this "treachery" with the fall of China and with the communization of Eastern Europe. There were logical and more probable explanations for everything that had happened but logic did not flourish in the last part of the decade of the forties or the early fifties.

Harry Truman was incredibly maladroit in handling the situation. First, he tried to dismiss it by labeling the communist exposés in Congress as a "red herring" designed to distract public attention from what he regarded as Democratic progressivism and Republican obstructionism. A case could be made for his position. There was no doubt that many Republicans and conservative Southern Democrats were using the communist issue to discredit the New Deal of Franklin D. Roosevelt. But regardless of the motives for the investigations, the fact remained that the investigators had brought to public attention the presence of secret communists in the federal government. To a large portion of the politically effective public, he sounded like a man trying to cover up a scandal by the use of pejorative language and by attacking the character of his opponents rather than the issue they were raising.

Unfortunately, Harry S Truman in terms of public perception was enshrouded with an aura of crooked big-city ward politics. He was probably the most rigidly honest President ever placed in the White House. But he was also a product of the Pendergast machine in Kansas City and he refused to repudiate any of his friends even though many of them—whether fairly or unfairly—looked like cartoon caricatures of paving-brick contract, ballot-box-stuffing politicians. It was fairly common for big-city political bosses to place men of integrity in nomination for the U.S. Senate. This meant that voters would concentrate on the top of the ticket and pay little attention to the jobs that really interested the machine—such as City Sealer or Commissioner of Weights and Measures. Such knowledge, however, was a bit too sophisticated for most Americans. They insisted on a ward-style political interpretation for every move made by Mr. Truman and this meant to far too many people that he was opposed to the exposé of communists because he wanted to save the Democratic Party from embarrassment.

To anyone who had to deal with the situation—whether as a journalist or a political adviser—it was impossible to avoid the realization that much of the anti-communist fury was directed at elite groups rather than at communists. There were a number of sources for this feeling. Ethnic discrimination in the 1920s and earlier had been fierce and no one was exempt from it except the white Anglo-Saxon Protestants and their descendants. Not all the WASPs, however, were in the elite group.

They included small, Middle Western farmers who were fundamentalist, rather than Anglican, in their religion and who bitterly resented what they called "the Eastern snobs." They could unite with the ethnic groups on one issue—opposition to what came to be known as "The Eastern Establishment." This was a concept difficult to define but, generally speaking, it covered men and women who had been educated in the Ivy League schools that patterned their curricula, to some extent, upon the British model.

It was not at all difficult to tie the so-called Eastern Establishment to the communists. In the mid-1930s, the communist movement became a focal point for American intellectuals. Many college students joined the Young Communist League and their elders went into organizations that were controlled by the Communist Party but that were not legally a part of the Communist Party. This movement had nothing to do with the communism of Marx, Lenin, and Stalin. It came about because of the Spanish civil war, which most intellectuals regarded as a testing ground for Fascist and Nazi aggression. They became embroiled in a communist organization because no one else seemed to be offering effective support to the People's Front government that opposed General Francisco Franco. After the war, when it became apparent that the communist record in Spain had been one of treachery, most of them dropped out. A substantial number had become so deeply embroiled that they remained under communist influence. This meant that when the investigations of communism started, the spotlight fell almost automatically on writers, actors, musicians, and government officials. There were not very many of them, but they were prominent, which made them look like a host of conspirators. Many of them had never been near an Ivy League college but that did not stop the anti-communists from putting them into that classification.

This should have been helpful to Harry S Truman. No one could possibly have accused him of being an Ivy League elitist. He was the quintessential "man next door"—the farm boy who could plow the straightest furrow in his county; the rough-talking artillery lieutenant; the small-town businessman who had gone bankrupt during the Depression. There was no way in which he could be classified as a Harvard don or an agitprop (Communist functionary) in a communist cell. Unfortunately, he had reacted to his conference with Josef Stalin in Potsdam by describing him as "good old Joe." And he had a Secretary of State, Dean Acheson, who looked as though he had just stepped out of a cartoon lampooning a "striped pants, cookie-pushing" diplomat. In reality, Acheson was almost obsessively anti-communist. But that didn't matter. He was cultured, aloof, precise in his speech, and looked like a snob. He did not "suffer a fool gladly"—an important art for anyone who deals with the public. Truman had set up a series of programs that did more to halt the expansion of the Soviet Union than anything else in the post–World War II years. But that didn't matter either. The fall of China to Mao Tse-tung was a blanket that excused anyone in the anti-communist movement from looking further.

Truman was totally incapable of propitiating the anti-communists. Even a loyalty check program for the State Department, which he instituted, failed to quiet the storm. It was the Korean War, however, that reduced him to near impotence.

There is no need to review the history of that war here.

What is important in considering its relationship with American politics is that it could not be "won" in the terms in which that word is usually understood. The objective was to bring the state of affairs back to what it was before the fighting started—an objective that is described in diplomatic language as the *status quo ante*. When the realization finally seeped through to the American people that their young men were dying for the *status quo ante,* the war became untenable. It was not a prize for which people were willing to sacrifice. When MacArthur said he had a way of winning the war, however risky, his words were electrifying. People were ready to hand him the country, and the only time in my life that I ever felt my government to be fragile consisted of the days I spent checking him into Washington for the United Press when Truman recalled him from Korea. Had he said "give it to me" when he walked past the White House on this occasion, the adoring crowds that thronged the streets might have done just that.

The Russell hearings defanged MacArthur. Upon examination, his plan for winning meant a major risk of a war with China and possibly the Soviet Union. No one was ready for that. But the hearings did not improve Mr. Truman's standing with the American people. If anything, they made things worse. Russell probed day after day to determine whether there was a military leader who would say the war could be "won." All of them declined to say so. The best they could promise was pushing the North Koreans back over the dividing line between the two countries. In other words, they would fight to a stalemate.

It is possible that Russell's skillful handling of the hearings averted a disaster. But it did not halt the erosion of confidence in the administration. Harry Truman's poll standings shrank to all-time lows and the government became, for all practical purposes, a caretaker operation. The man at the top could no longer give it direction. He could only exacerbate antagonisms.

One of the most important functions of a President lies in his capacity to set the nation's political agenda. He is the person who, at the beginning of every year, determines the topics for public debate and the conditions under which the popular dialogue will be conducted. Of course, Congress and the courts can modify his proposals, substitute others for them, or reject them altogether. And, of course, unforeseen events can force a revision of all his plans. But to the extent that the political agenda *can* be controlled by human planning, the power lies in his hands. He has the initiative and can always start a ball rolling without consulting others. Congress is too unwieldy a body to attempt more than an occasional initiative and the courts can act only upon cases that are brought before them.

During the last two years of his administration, Mr. Truman lost the power to control the agenda. His appropriations were chopped to shreds; his initiatives were pigeonholed often without even formal consideration; his appointees were given short shrift. The nation floated in limbo without anything to hold it together other than the federal bureaucracy—a group of men and women with a higher degree of efficiency than is usually conceded to them but without the ability—and usually even without the desire—to strike out on new trails.

Of course, the forms of political debate continued. But

they consisted of nothing other than men and women going through motions because they had nothing else to do. Nobody expected anything to happen and it didn't. Liberals and conservatives excoriated each other furiously. Ideologues made "educational" speeches on their pet projects. Except for the passage of routine appropriation bills, however, there was no action. Everyone was waiting.

What they were waiting for was the election of a President who had no ties to the past. The Democratic Party— or, at least, the Democratic Party of Harry S Truman— was perceived as an alliance of sleazy crooks and soft-headed idealists who were easily manipulated by the Communist Party. This did not necessarily mean a switch to the Republican Party, as became apparent in 1952 when a Republican Presidential landslide produced only thin Republican majorities in the Congress. But what it definitely meant was a desire for a leader who could not be associated with either communist fellow-traveling or small-time graft.

In retrospect, Mr. Truman might have been better off if the scandals uncovered in his administration had been of greater magnitude. They were incredibly small-time. Historians of the future may have trouble understanding how the public could become so excited over bribes that went no further than a mink coat or a Polaroid camera or a deep freeze. It was the very smallness that made them so troublesome. The boodle boys of the era had no grandeur whatsoever. They could not even excite the admiration that some still feel for the big-time pirates such as Blackbeard or Captain Kidd.

In looking back over this period, I have come to the

conclusion that it offered us an important lesson in the workings of the American government. It is that our whole system depends for its success upon the *unifying* qualities of the President. Much more important than his skill in managing our affairs is his skill in keeping us together as a nation. This is of supreme concern in a democracy, where the political, social, and economic forces are in a constant state of change and frequently become so fragmented that they tend to drive us apart rather than hold us together.

As leader of a reasonably unified nation, Mr. Truman might have been a very successful Chief Executive who would have retired from the position to plaudits from all quarters. He had the misfortune to preside during an era when our country was in an accelerated state of change brought into being by World War II. Power was slipping rapidly from the grip of the big-city machines; the South was in the throes of industrialization, bringing unionization in its wake; mobility had become the watchword of the day with people moving from city to city and from job to job; areas like Long Island, which had once been the haven for duck producers and wealthy commuters, had become a bedroom for a major metropolis. And the returning GIs were restive—anxious to make up for the years spent in uniform and totally outside the system that had produced the likes of Harry Truman.

This was a period in which a managerial President or a crusading President was bound to be frustrated. A democracy can be managed only when it is possible to assemble coalitions behind programs. Such coalitions were simply not in the cards. People who are on the move do not unite. They will respond only to unifying symbols that are designed to hold them together rather than spur them to action. Mr. Truman enjoyed fighting far too much to be such a unifying symbol.

One cannot help but wonder what would have happened had the Republicans nominated a "true Republican" (which meant a partisan conservative) to the Presidency in 1952. My guess is that he would probably have won—not because of his popularity but because Mr. Truman was probably beyond redemption in the polls and would pass on his liabilities to any Democratic successor. But I believe he would have run into the same conditions that plagued his predecessor—an inability to put coalitions together. In my judgment, it was not Mr. Truman's liberalism that led to his downfall but his combative partisanship. His courage and his willingness to fight against all odds made him very attractive as a man. But it did not do very much to calm the country.

I was a rather partisan Democrat myself in those days and in 1952 was fully convinced that civilization would come to an end in 1952 if Adlai Stevenson, the Democratic nominee, did not win. When I look back from the vantage point of political experience, it becomes obvious that Dwight D. Eisenhower was tailor-made for the times. I later came to know Mr. Stevenson quite well and believe that in many respects he was a better man. But even though he was less partisan than Truman, he was not the person to bring the nation the unity it so badly needed. Dwight D. Eisenhower is unlikely to be remembered in terms of the reverential awe that surrounds Washington, Lincoln, or Franklin D. Roosevelt. He should be remembered, however, for being the man who was on the spot when we needed him and no one else was available.

His Kansas boyhood gave him impeccable "grass roots" credentials. But no one could consider him an untutored "hick." He had dignity that was devoid of arrogance and geniality that was above the level of the booster-boy handshake. He looked not only honest but honorable and nothing about him spelled sleaze. His most important attribute, however, was that he had held a number of political positions that the public did not regard as political. As Commander in Chief of the Allied forces in western Europe, his principal task had been to hold the Allies together. As Supreme Commander of the NATO forces in Europe, he had to maintain serenity in the midst of some of the most explosive temperaments in recent history—including that of Charles de Gaulle. Again, he had passed with flying colors. Finally, he had been head of Columbia University, which meant that he was plunged into the swirl of academic politics, compared to which Presidential politics is a Sunday school picnic. Again, he passed with flying colors and the assignment may even have been helpful to him by giving a civilian coloration to his military career.

Finally, there was the fact that, historically, he was associated with all the victories and none of the defeats. This was especially important when the American people were fighting a war in Korea that could not be won. He fitted into the White House so naturally that it was never really a contest. The best Adlai Stevenson could do was to preserve the dignity of the Democratic Party. But it was Dwight D. Eisenhower who brought to a close in 1952 an era of dissension and who, without intending to do so, set the stage upon which Lyndon B. Johnson was to perform so successfully.

5

To a Worldwide Role

The Senate of the 1950s can be understood only against the background of the conversion of the United States from isolationism to internationalism. Both terms need definition, as it is difficult for anyone who did not have some adult life before World War II to recognize either approach as a philosophy. To the present generation, the fierce arguments that swept the nation during that period would be utterly ridiculous. In modern times, we have arguments as to whether specific foreign policies are wise and over the extent to which we should commit our resources to implementing them. But it would be difficult to find any group of Americans who would argue today that we should have no foreign policy at all. That is something of an exaggeration but not much. The isolationists were against any system of dealing with other countries that involved obligations on our part.

The "no alliances" theory was more than a conversation piece before World War II. It was a respectable concept held by many of the most respected political leaders in the nation. Their names are now forgotten. But Senators such as William Borah of Idaho; Hiram Johnson of California; Bennett Champ Clark of Missouri; Robert M. LaFollette, Jr., of Wisconsin; and Burton K. Wheeler of Montana, all of whom were isolationists, dominated foreign policy in the United States Senate. It should be added that all of them commanded nationwide recognition because of their association with the Progressive movement, which, to young liberals and academics, was the only attractive feature of the political scene in the 1920s. I can still feel the shivers of awe that went down my spine when I, as a very young reporter fresh from college, approached them for interviews.

There were many deep roots to the concept. The isolationist leaders traced their intellectual ancestry back to George Washington and his farewell address to Congress—the one in which he warned against the entangling alliances. It is doubtful in my mind, however, that a statement that no one today reads except as an assignment in a college history class could serve to found such a powerful political force. In the early days of our Republic there was no particular attraction to foreign adventures. We were too busy settling the lands west of the Appalachians, and the oceans really were an effective bar to the kind of potential invasions that usually cause nations to think in terms of forming defensive alliances. Later, when we entered the industrial age, there was a burning desire to foster the growth of our factories by shutting out foreign competition. The isolationism bred by high tariffs easily extended itself to the political field.

World War I represented no real break in the concept. We entered the war because we were persuaded that we were defending ourselves against German aggression (those who wish to explore this point further are advised to look up the "Zimmermann telegram" and the sinking of the *Lusitania*). Woodrow Wilson had been reelected on a platform of keeping us out of the war and changed his mind only on the basis of what was presented to the nation as extreme provocation. The true heart of the people is better revealed in our refusal to join the League of Nations after the war was over rather than our willingness to fight when it was on. To the powers who controlled the Senate and to their constituencies at home, it was one thing to fight; it was another thing altogether to join in an alliance. The League of Nations to them was the very type of activity against which George Washington warned.

The World War I experience may well have strengthened, rather than lessened, the isolationist concept in the United States. This is due to the fact that, in the American mind, it established Great Britain as the symbol of international dealings. The 1920s and 1930s were the decades in which ethnic groups, which previously had restricted their political activities to cities, made enormous gains in national influence. Virtually all of them—the Irish, the Italians, the Germans, the Poles, and the Czechs—nursed ancestral grievances against "Perfidious Albion" (I am quoting my fourth-grade Irish schoolteacher who was quite typical of the instructors in the Chicago public school system) and wanted "no truck" with the English. To this should be added the anti-war intellectual movement, which wanted no part of any agreement that could end in fighting.

By the early thirties, many influential Americans regarded World War I as a mistake, and theories that we were "tricked" into it became quite common. On college campuses, students assembled to take the Oxford oath—a pledge that they would not support their country in any war. In Congress a Senator named Gerald P. Nye, from North Dakota, headed an investigation that wound up blaming "munitions makers" for the collapse of disarmament programs in the twenties. The hearings also resulted in the passage of a law that the United States would not ship arms to either side in a conflict in which it was neutral. The final goal of the isolationists was not reached. It was to secure an amendment to the Constitution (sponsored by Representative Louis Ludlow of Indiana) that would require a nationwide plebiscite before the United States could enter a war.

The tactical strength of the isolationists was enhanced by their service as "shock troops" for Franklin D. Roosevelt when he first became President. Their Progressive backgrounds put them in complete sympathy with the social legislation sponsored by the New Deal. This led to something of an anomaly at a later date when foreign policy—to participate or not to participate in World War II—became the principal item of discussion on America's political agenda. Many of those who wanted to go in on the side of Great Britain early were men of a conservative stripe from New England or the Southern cotton and tobacco states. The theories of isolation had never been popular in those regions, where the importance of international trade was recognized.

Foreign policy did not figure as too much of an issue in the early days of the New Deal because domestic social concerns dominated the nation. The arms embargo was passed easily by Congress in 1935 because no one who might be internationalist saw it as having any major impact. There were some agonizing moments among liberals when they discovered that it prevented the United States from helping the Popular Front government during the Spanish civil war. But the agony did not last too long. In 1934, Roosevelt had suggested in a speech in Chicago that democracies should combine to "quarantine the aggressors"—by which he meant Germany, Italy, and Japan. The statement had such an unfavorable reception that he soon dropped it. The isolationists were clearly in the saddle—so much so that they turned FDR down flat in the early summer of 1939 when he asked that the Congress repeal the arms embargo and substitute a "cash and carry" law. The request was made of Congressional leaders at a private meeting in the White House where he said that war was about ready to break out in Europe and the United States needed more flexibility. Senator Borah replied bluntly that he had better information than the President and there would be no war in Europe that year. At the time, Senator Borah had more credibility on foreign policy with the public than did the President. Congress adjourned without taking any action on the issue. When Germany invaded Poland a few months later in 1939 the Borah credibility was somewhat dented. But the fact still remained that the United States could not even supply weapons to either side, let alone be a participant. Under the law, we could only be spectators unless we were ready to declare war ourselves.

The arms issue was crucial. Germany had spent years

preparing at full speed for the conflict. England and France, on the other hand, had made only a half-hearted effort. The result was that Germany started out with a complete arsenal that could be used to seize virtually the entire manufacturing area of Europe. Unless the British and the French could secure armaments from somewhere, the outcome of the war was a foregone conclusion. The only conceivable "somewhere" was the United States. To keep the total arms embargo on the statute books was to virtually assure Nazi domination of Europe.

President Roosevelt called a special session of the Congress in the fall of 1939 to repeal the arms embargo. It was not until many years later that I recognized the political acumen with which he handled the move. Borah, the acknowledged leader of the isolationists, had suffered a loss of prestige that extended to all of his followers because of his invalid prophecy in the early summer. This meant that the "internationalists" (which, as soon as the war broke out, meant Americans who wanted the British and French to win) had a slight edge. However, it was only a slight edge and if they overplayed the hand, it would evaporate quickly. Asking only for repeal of the arms embargo would have been an overplay and the measure could well have been defeated. So the request for ending the embargo was accompanied by a condition that any nation buying munitions from us would have to pay cash and supply its own means of transportation. FDR's estimate of what Congress would and would not swallow turned out to be right on the button. His request was granted.

As I have already stated, the debate became deadly dull after a few days. There was a brief period in which the oratorical stars of the Senate—Borah, Vandenberg, Pittman, and Connally—really shone. Those four, whose appearances were scheduled almost to the minute, said everything that anyone was willing to say on the issues. All of the following speakers offered only variations on their themes. There was another aspect to the debate, however, that did more to contribute to its monotony than did the secondary talents of the agonists. It was the simple fact that they were not talking about the real issues. Both sides were claiming to espouse a course that would keep the United States out of the war in Europe. The true bone of contention was whether the United States would tilt the scales in the war. To turn the President down was to guarantee Germany, Italy, and Japan victory. To accede to the President's request was to give England and France a fighting chance. The logic was inexorable.

To say that logic is inexorable, however, is not to say that it is recognized. There was little doubt in my mind as a reporter covering the debate that the "internationalists" realized from the beginning that they were seeking to put our country on the side of the Allies. They did not, however, realize that the war had gone too far for us to intervene in any fashion without going in eventually to fight. The isolationists, on the other hand, did not, at first, recognize that they were calling for a policy that would help Nazism and Fascism. Both were quite sincere in their protestations of love for peace. The result was that the debate overall sounded a false note but a note whose fallacy could not be readily identified.

The repeal of the arms embargo was followed by a series of measures, each one of which brought us a step closer to siding with Great Britain. The turning point was the Lend-Lease debate. Here the objective was clearly to come out on the British side. When it was coupled with the Selective Service Act the issue became clear. We were preparing not only to help but to enter the fighting. The Rooseveltian sense of timing was superb and had no equal in later years until Lyndon Johnson entered the White House. Like FDR, he could sense precisely how far Congress could be pushed on a measure and could lay plans for pushing it even further. In the pre–World War II case, FDR also demonstrated how to get things done when Congressional action was impossible. For example, when the British badly needed more destroyers to protect their cargoes from German submarines, he arranged to swap fifty "over age" American destroyers for rights to naval bases in the Caribbean. The deal was consummated before the legislators could do anything to stop it. On another occasion, he used his powers as Commander in Chief of the Armed Forces to have our navy escort convoys to England halfway across the Atlantic where they would be picked up by British escorts for the rest of the journey. In effect, this was virtually doubling the size of the British navy.

Meanwhile, the Senate debate was accompanied by a public debate that was one of the most passionate in our history. Organizations sprang up all over the country— the America First Committee, the Keep America Out of War Committee, the Mothers of America, and many others. The isolationist groups were the most frenzied simply because they sensed from the beginning that they were being outmaneuvered and they streamed into Washington in numbers that were not matched until the civil rights debates of the 1950s. There was pent-up fury among them that exploded from time to time—fortunately without doing any personal injury. One of the "mothers' " organizations hung Senator Claude Pepper of Florida in effigy in the park across from the Capitol plaza, and there were a number of purse-swinging demonstrations in the building itself. As time went on, it became apparent that anti-Semitism was one of the underpinnings of the isolationists in the public debate. At first it manifested itself only in speeches blaming "the international bankers" for trying to bring the United States into the war. But the audiences who heard those speeches were not interested in bankers. They translated the phrase into "Jews" and anyone who sat in their audiences did not have to exercise imaginative powers to know what they meant.

I do not know whether any of the isolationist Senators were actual anti-Semites. My sense of smell made me suspicious of a few of them. But the closest to an overt act committed in the Senate was an investigation of charges that the movie industry was propagandizing the United States to enter the war. The obvious intent was to parade before the public a number of Jewish names associated with the motion pictures. Whether this would have made any impact is problematical. We will never know because it turned out that Senator Gerald P. Nye, who had introduced the resolution for the investigation, had never seen any of the pictures himself. This made the whole investigation appear so ridiculous that it was dropped.

Whatever may have been the reality, however, the isolationist cause became identified with Nazism once we entered the war. Only a few of the isolationist leaders had repudiated anti-Semitism. And once we were actually fighting, the logic of their position became clear. They *had* espoused a course that would have been helpful to Hitler, Mussolini, and Tojo, and the fact that their motives may have been pure did not count—as it hardly ever counts— in the realm of public debate. However, the fact that isolationism was no longer popular as a *word* did not mean that it had become unpopular as a *cause*. It continued to live a sort of underground life and did not really surface until the 1950s. Much of what happened needs this background to be comprehensible.

In the 1950s, Congressional action—sparked by the Senate—became famous because it resulted in the passage of so many social laws. A Republican President and a Democratic Congress managed to put together legislation in the fields of housing, health, social security, education, and many others that had few precedents since the early days of the New Deal. The debates, however, did not center on those issues. The true course of the Senate during the decade was the running debate over foreign policy and over civil rights. These were the two great issues that dominated the scene. The civil rights issue will be and has been discussed in other works. For the moment, our concentration will be centered on the foreign policy issues that actually revived the isolationist-internationalist debates that preceded World War II.

The language had changed but the same patterns reasserted themselves. Both the internationalists and the isolationists had claimed in the thirties that they were trying to keep America out of war. In the 1950s, the two groups both claimed that they were internationalists trying to keep communism from dominating the world. The one-time isolationists saw the danger in China, however, and

73

the one-time internationalists saw it in Europe. There was a significant difference in the people conducting the debate that should be noted here. In the years that had intervened since Pearl Harbor, the Republican Party had made a considerable comeback in the Congress. Most of it had involved the areas of the nation that were fundamentally isolationist—the Middle West and the Rocky Mountain states. As a consequence, Dwight D. Eisenhower found himself facing an agonizing dilemma when he became President in 1953.

Eisenhower's Republicanism was probably more an affinity with the nation's business leaders than anything else. There is no evidence that he was deeply ideological in any sense of the word and he could have been nominated on the Democratic ticket and run for the Presidency in 1952 on the basis of the same speeches that he made from GOP platforms. He had an extremely high degree of political ability in terms of finding unifying themes that held people together and led them into action. But in terms of identifying and embracing political goals it is doubtful whether he thought in any terms other than applying common sense to the achievement of decency and efficiency in government. This may well have been his biggest asset. The American people needed a rest after the super-heated ideological battles of the Truman administration, and Ike gave it to them.

The Republican Congress—and especially the Republican Senate—at that point *was* highly ideological in the field of foreign policy. In the late 1940s, there had been a remarkable degree of unity in Congress on programs to strengthen Western Europe and the Middle East against Soviet Union expansionism. The "do-nothing, good-for-nothing Eightieth Congress," against which Truman had inveighed so effectively in 1948, had actually approved all his requests in the international field, including such unprecedented moves as the Marshall Plan and the Greek-Turkish aid program. Furthermore, the spark plug for the North Atlantic Treaty Organization (NATO), which became the keystone of U.S. foreign policy, was a Republican pre-war isolationist—Arthur Vandenberg. This Irenic state of affairs did not survive very long. By the time Ike took the oath of office, the isolationists had a very strong foothold in the Senate. This time, however, they had a totally different rationale for their position and avoided the tag name altogether. To be identified as an isolationist was not a very good stance in a nation that connected the term with pro-Nazism.

The neo-isolationism of the 1950s was built on a theory of history that held that the Soviet hegemony over Eastern Europe and the fall of China to Mao Tse-tung after World War II had been the result of treachery in the United States government. In its crudest form, the theory was that men such as Alger Hiss and Harry Dexter White (an assistant Secretary of the Treasury who had participated in international monetary conferences) had induced the United States to make agreements that enhanced communist power on the world scene. As Hiss had been a top American functionary at the founding conference of the United Nations, the world organization was regarded with deep suspicion and some very important agreements made under its auspices—the Genocide Convention and the Human Rights Covenant, for example—were shelved. (Only this year—thirty-seven years after it was submitted—did the United States Senate approve,

83–11, the United Nations treaty that outlaws genocide.)

An important underpinning of the neo-isolationist theories was the concept that China had fallen to communism because the United States had placed pressure upon Chiang Kai-shek to form an alliance with the Chinese communists. The very obvious fact that Chiang's graft-ridden regime was simply unable to hold the Chinese people together was ignored. And when Chiang eventually abandoned mainland China and took his remaining military forces to Formosa, he established one of the major issues in domestic American politics of the 1950s. The reason was that the move provided an ideal "cover" for isolationism. Obvious isolationists could easily claim that they were "internationalists" but were not going to vote for measures to help European democracies unless equal consideration was given to Chiang.

For Eisenhower, this attitude of the Republican leadership in both the House and the Senate was an excruciating problem. He had been a major part of the formation of foreign policy under two Democratic Presidents. He had been the Supreme Commander of the NATO forces in Europe and had been called in by Truman time and again for consultations and, according to a story widely circulated in Washington, on one of those occasions he was offered Truman's support for the Democratic Presidential nomination. In securing the Republican Presidential nomination, he had defeated the isolationist wing of the GOP. Now he was President of the United States under a party label that also covered legislators who wanted him to repudiate everything that had been done. Under the circumstances, he was more than willing to take part in an alliance with the Congressional Democrats to prevent the dismantling of the whole post–World War II structure of foreign policy that had been built by the United States.

The word "alliance," as applied to Eisenhower and the Democrats, must be used with a high degree of caution. As far as I know, it was never confirmed at any meeting. (I believe I would have known from my vantage point as director of the Senate Democratic Policy Committee.) The reality was a group of highly sensitive politicians who knew how to make and keep agreements without putting anything in writing or even conferring with one another. Obviously, Eisenhower welcomed Democratic help in salvaging a foreign policy that he himself helped make. Obviously, the Democrats were willing to proffer that help as a means of clearing the record of Democratic Presidents. There were a few "fringe" benefits that went along with the "deal" that was never made but which was just as binding as though it had been chiseled in stone on Mount Rushmore. The Democrats gained Eisenhower's acquiescence in passing bills that had a Democratic coloration to them. Eisenhower gained immunity from the type of partisan attacks that one would normally expect from Democrats in Congress against a Republican President. Of course, the bills could not go too far in the Democratic direction (at this point, meaning a liberal, social direction) without running into an effective veto. And, of course, Eisenhower appointees became targets for attacks that normally would have been directed at their chief. But as long as everyone lived by a "rule of reason," everyone was happy except the Congressional Republicans and the would-be Democratic Presidential candidates.

The first overt result of the "understanding" (or possibly the first event that brought it about) surfaced in 1953 at the opening session of Congress. One of the major goals of the neo-isolationists had been to secure a repudiation of the various agreements that were made at Yalta, Potsdam, and other World War II conferences of the victorious Allies. These were allegedly the source of the fall of Poland and other nations of Eastern Europe to the Soviet Union. Eisenhower had made a somewhat vague promise that he would do something about it and once he was installed in office, the Congressional Republicans put pressure on him to comply with the promise. The pressure put him in a difficult spot. The agreements had all been made in terms of the presence of Allied troops at the time. Obviously, the Soviets could control any area in which they had forces and we could control any in which we had forces. The lines that were drawn were based on practicalities. What was even more important, however, was that our post–World War II presence in Western Europe was based legally upon the agreements. To have repudiated them unilaterally would have handed the Soviet Union an important forensic weapon in urging our departure. It was a tough spot to be in and Eisenhower attempted to find his way out of it by sending Congress a resolution denouncing Soviet violations of the agreements.

Senate Republicans, headed by Robert A. Taft, made it clear at once that they felt betrayed. In the Senate's Foreign Relations Committee, the Republican clerks started drawing up amendments to repudiate the agreements themselves. Lyndon B. Johnson put an end to the activity by calling a meeting of the Senate Democratic Policy Committee and passing a resolution to endorse the Eisenhower position. He made it clear that the Democrats would insist on upholding the President's hand by endorsing his language without changing a comma. To change the wording of the resolution, he charged, would give the rest of the world a feeling that the United States was not united in the struggle against communism. The picture before the public was that of a great war hero and a very popular President under attack by a disruptive Republican Party while a constructive Democratic Party was rushing to his defense. Taft was a realist. The whole issue was dropped. But it became the basis for the Democratic strategy that dominated the entire eight years of the Eisenhower administration.

The pattern was repeated over and over again. The Republican Party was not isolationist nationally. However, its isolationist wing was strong in the Congress. Therefore, it had a tendency to oppose Eisenhower on almost anything he did in the foreign policy field. There was a long string of issues—the Human Rights Covenant, the Genocide Convention, the Status of Forces treaties, the Southeast Asia Treaty Organization, aid to Lebanon. On all of them, the opposition centered on the Senate GOP. Both Senate leaders of the party—Taft and William Knowland, of California—during that period were generally against the President. In effect, they were ideal patsies for the shrewd Democratic leaders headed by Lyndon B. Johnson.

The result of all this was that the Democrats rode piggyback on the Eisenhower popularity and the Republicans suffered loss after loss in the Congress. The 1952 election that placed Eisenhower in the White House had given the Republicans a slight majority in both houses of Congress. This evaporated in 1954 and the Democrats were back in control by a slight margin. This was extended in 1956 and the 1958 election brought in the largest Democratic Congressional majorities since the palmy days of the New Deal. It was a major paradox that could happen only in the politics of the United States.

Johnson took advantage of the situation to build a "Democratic record." Most of this was based on gaining increases in appropriations requested by the President for programs that had been passed during Democratic Presidential administrations. The basic strategy was to increase such appropriations or authorizations to a point where they would be fought by Congressional Republicans but not to a point where they would draw a White House veto. The major concentration was in such areas as health, social security, housing, education, and social services. In other areas—such as civil rights—great care was exercised to operate on the Presidential requests rather than to initiate legislation. During the entire decade, the only bill that really originated with the Congressional Democrats was the Outer Space Act, which was a Lyndon Johnson promotion. He was careful to get Eisenhower approval before the final passage of the measure.

The high-water mark of the isolationist surge in the 1950s came upon what was known as the Bricker amendment, named after its sponsor John W. Bricker, a Senator from Ohio. Today he is one of the most totally forgotten politicians in American history. But in the late forties and early fifties, he was regarded in many quarters as Presidential material. This was largely due to his appearance. He was a handsome man with a beautifully coiffed thatch of white hair. In some respects, he resembled Warren G. Harding, although he had much finer features. It was his proposal to amend the Constitution, however, rather than his Presidential suitability or his good looks that made him a major figure of the decade.

There was a deceptive simplicity to the Bricker amendment. It merely said that no unconstitutional law could be made constitutional by giving it a treaty umbrella. Early in this century, the Congress had passed an act regulating the hunting of migratory game birds, such as ducks and geese. The measure was based on the theory that the birds were in passage from state to state and therefore came under the Interstate Commerce Clause of the Constitution and could be protected by the federal government. The courts held the law invalid and rested upon an older doctrine that awarded the title of wild game to the land that it occupied. That meant that each state could enact its own regulations. The federal government then concluded a treaty with Canada and Congress again passed the regulatory law on the theory that it was necessary to carry out the provisions of the treaty. This time, the courts upheld the law.

There was a widely believed story in Washington that Bricker became interested in the question when he was arrested for shooting ducks over a baited area and against the federal law. That, of course, was not the reason he gave for his amendment. Instead, he concentrated on all the things that he claimed could happen to our Constitution under the treaty power. He raised specters of foreign troops being quartered on American soil; of American soldiers being subjected to cruel punishments in other lands; of Americans being punished by other nations for not treating all its ethnic groups exactly alike. All of this, he said, could and probably would happen if his amendment was not adopted. Some of his greatest strength arose from the claim that "socialized medicine" would be brought to the United States against the popular will if the Covenant of Human Rights treaty was approved before the Bricker amendment. This brought the doctors into the fray on his side.

In the 1950s, doctors were one of the most potent political forces in the United States. They had a prestige all out of proportion to their numbers. This arose from their close relationship with their patients during the era of house calls and from their position in many communities as social leaders. Unfortunately for them, their political potency was matched by political naïveté. To put it bluntly, they could be taken into camp by any clever operator who promised to save them from the dread apparition of socialized medicine. They weren't quite sure what it was but they knew they were "agin it."

With the doctors behind it, an incredible momentum built up behind the Bricker amendment. Senators and Representatives received thousands of letters every day from their home districts. The hand of the physicians was apparent in almost all of them. Under the onslaught, the ranks of opposition crumpled. It soon became apparent that the two-thirds majority needed to pass a Constitutional amendment through the Senate had been reached. No one really knew what it would do. Large numbers of Senators and Representatives were afraid of it. But there was no hope of stopping it through direct opposition, regardless of the questionable nature of the proposal. Eisenhower remained aloof from the legislative battle on the grounds that Presidents do not participate in the amending processes of the Constitution. The machinery of the

House of Represetatives was too clumsy for it to be stopped in that chamber. Obviously, the only possibility was legislative maneuvering.

The Senate leadership finally persuaded Senator Walter F. George of Georgia to offer a substitute amendment. In effect, it said that all laws had to comply with the Constitution. However, it said it in words that sounded very much like the language of the Bricker amendment. Among conservatives, George was a much more highly respected name than Bricker. He had been the first target in FDR's "purge campaign" of 1938 and his successful battle against Roosevelt had made him something of a legend. Basically, the Democratic leadership maneuver was to provide a safe harbor to which Senators could flee who felt uneasy about the Bricker amendment but who also felt compelled to vote for it under constituent pressure. The maneuver worked. Enough votes were garnered to substitute George for Bricker.

At that point, sanity reasserted itself. The substitution snapped the mystique that had made the Bricker amendment so unbeatable. In the final vote, the George amendment fell just short of the two-thirds majority necessary for passage. The whole concept went down the drain. Also down the drain went the strength of the isolationists and the strength of the medical lobby. The doctors had made the classic mistake of using their power for something that basically was none of their business—the unforgivable sin in legislative thinking. Since that date, the profession has received short shrift from the House of Representatives and the Senate of the United States.

The Bricker amendment is now mercifully forgotten— as it should be. But it is worth recounting here because it was the most dramatic incident in a running political battle that served to enhance, rather than diminish, the efficiency and productivity of the United States Senate. The isolationists, contrary to their desires, actually forged a form of arm's-length cooperation between the President of the United States and the Democratic Congressional leadership. Skillful and sensitive leadership can surmount political obstacles and even turn them to advantage.

6

The Cast of Characters

The four years of Presidential impotence had created in the Senate a structure that resembled China under the warlords. The nominal majority leaders—Scott W. Lucas of Illinois and Ernest W. McFarland of Arizona—had no control whatsoever. They were able men who had proven themselves in past political battles. The members of the Senate treated them politely and saw to it that all the forms of parliamentary procedure were observed. Both, however, had even less authority than Chiang Kai-shek. What power there was rested in the hands of four or five men who knew how to put together the other fragments of the body into a force that could block the passage of anything they didn't like.

The men of power were also men of exceptional ability. In any organization other than the Senate, they would have been unchallenged leaders capable of leading their cohorts to victory after victory. The problem was that they found themselves teamed up with men of equal capacity and equal determination and had no overriding unification principle to bring them together. There were simply not enough followers for the leaders. Recalling those days, I can still wince when I hear someone say that "America needs leadership." There is always leadership. But there are many times when there is a lack of followership and this was one of those times.

At the apex of the heap were two men with the most massive intellects I have ever encountered. They were Eugene Millikin of Colorado and Richard B. Russell of Georgia. Either man could have gone into any university and taught with distinction: Millikin—law, economics, or political science; Russell—law, history, or political science. At the same time, however, they were intensely practical politicians who knew how to extract every vote from their constituents and who invariably emerged on top in the rough-and-tumble "King of the Mountain" game that characterizes so much of American politics.

Millikin had an earthy sense of humor that delighted the whole press corps even though very few stories were written about him. This was by his own choice. He had mastered a number of techniques to keep his name out of stories in which he was the principal actor. One of his ploys was the use of profanity, which could not be printed. Asked about a difficult situation, he would invariably reply: "I'm going to paint my ass white and run with the antelopes." There was one period in which he was chairman of the Senate Finance Committee. The House counterpart was the Ways and Means Committee headed by Representative Daniel Reed of New York. The two were in fundamental disagreement about tax policies and Reed issued a stream of statements that amounted to challenges to his colleague. Millikin saw no sense to accepting the challenges and told reporters: "You are not going to get me into a pissing match with Dan Reed." By modern standards, such statements are relatively mild. But in the journalism of the late forties and the early fifties they were taboo. They could not even be paraphrased. At the same time, no one could say that he had refused to comment. Baffled reporters found they could do nothing but leave his name out of the stories altogether—which was precisely what he wanted.

As a young lawyer, Millikin had represented one of the figures in the famous Teapot Dome scandal and had emerged from the experience with considerable money. He was not a greedy man and he devoted the rest of his life to enjoying it. All of us had the feeling that he regarded the Senate as a gentleman's club, which he had joined for its companionship and intellectual stimulation. His colleague—Senator Edwin C. Johnson (no relation to Lyndon B.)—was also a Senate powerhouse, of somewhat lesser magnitude. The two men set up one of the coziest working relationships in the history of American politics even though Millikin was a Republican and Johnson a Democrat. At one time they even joined in splitting the salary and office expenses of an assistant whose sole job was to snare contracts for Colorado constituents. The assistant was instructed to give the credit to whomever needed it the most badly at any given moment. Under no circumstances would the two campaign against each other.

The immediate instrument of Millikin's power was his

dominating position on the Finance Committee. This group has jurisdiction over taxes and tariffs—two subjects in which Millikin was more of an expert than the staff technicians employed by the committee. Nothing *could* go through the committee against his opposition and anything reasonable *could* go through with his support. The fact that I have emphasized the word "could" should convey a message to the reader. No one in the Senate was going to select such a man as an enemy—particularly when he had the good sense not to exact impossible repayments from his colleagues for his support.

Although it is somewhat out of order in terms of this book, a Millikin story is worth repeating here. It was an incident that took place in 1955, after Lyndon Johnson's hold on the workings of the United States Senate had become quite firm. The Democrats had a clear majority but the Republican minority was still substantial and capable of blocking measures upon which the majority was not united. One such bill would provide for a dam in what was known as the Kicking Horse Canyon—a project that Democrats supported. It had been bottled up in committee, and in retaliation, the Democrats had put a hold on a Republican measure to develop the upper Colorado River.

Early in the year, Johnson had gone to the Mayo Clinic in Rochester, Minnesota, for removal of a kidney stone. After his return, he was approached by Millikin on the floor and the following dialogue took place:

"Lyndon, when you were at Mayo's, did they test your urine?" asked Millikin in his most pompous manner. Upon receiving an affirmative reply, he then asked:

"Tell me, Lyndon, what was the specific gravity?"

"I don't know, Senator," replied Johnson, "but they told me it was perfectly all right."

"Good, good. I'm glad to hear that it was first class," Millikin continued. "What was the albumen content?"

"I really don't know, Senator," replied Johnson, baffled and wondering whether Millikin was suffering from some kidney ailment that he wanted to discuss. "But they told me that it was perfectly all right."

"That's good, Lyndon," Millikin persisted. "I am glad to hear that the albumen content was also first class. How was the sugar content?"

Upon receiving the same assurances that everything was in order, Millikin uncorked the punch line of the conversation.

"Lyndon, you have just made me very happy in the reassurances about your urine. I have had so much of it in my face lately that I wanted to be sure it was first class. Now, can we have a little talk about the Colorado River and any legislative connections that are pertinent?"

Within a matter of weeks, both bills were scheduled for floor consideration later in the year.

I have coupled Millikin and Russell simply because of their fantastic brainpower. The two, however, were quite different. Millikin was a highly civilized man who sought to enjoy life and would do whatever was necessary to achieve his goals. He was not the kind of a political leader who would step into a situation merely because it needed to be resolved. He was meticulous in meeting his obligations to other people and he was willing to lend a helping hand as long as it did not require too much effort. But one could not think of him in terms of a cause. He was a superb politician to whom politics was only a part of his life.

Russell was of quite another stripe. It was impossible to think of him other than in terms of causes, and politics *was* his life.

Unlike Millikin, Russell did not go out of his way to keep his name from creeping into the press. He was quite capable, however, of deciding *how* it would appear in the press. He had no taste for publicity merely for the sake of publicity but thought it had utility in maintaining the support of constituents. His constituents were Georgians—largely rural, conservative, and segregationist. He was convinced that no one from a *Deep* South state could ever make a serious race for the Presidency—a race that would require a "national" image. As a result, the correspondents who covered the Senate saw only one side of the man—the leader of the battle for Southern causes, including the blockage of civil rights legislation.

Russell's opposition to civil rights legislation was as sincere as was his deep love for the South. There was another side to the man, however, which I had not anticipated. His distaste for civil rights legislation was accompanied by a conviction as deep as his love for Dixie that the American political system required both give and take from all parties. In his philosophy, everyone had to swallow a bitter pill at some stage of every debate on serious legislation. He had exercised every parliamentary wile at his command—and there were plenty of them—to prevent desegregation legislation from coming to a vote. As we were drawn closer together by the peculiar circumstances of our relationship during the MacArthur hearings, he began to talk to me about his views on other matters. It was then that I learned that he did not believe that the proponents of civil rights were really serious about their cause—that they were using it as a banner to attract constituents rather than as a practical means of solving a problem. I ultimately came to the conclusion that he would withdraw his opposition to a vote if the anti-segregationists gave him any indication that they were willing to trade back and forth on the issue. He would fight the legislation to the bitter end and go down fighting. But he would quash a filibuster so the Senate could vote. In 1957, he was given such evidence and my surmise turned out to be correct. The bill was passed with only one Southern Senator staging a filibuster—a grandstand play that lost him the friendship of his colleagues.

An even more surprising (to me) aspect of Russell's philosophy was his feeling that the South had to take steps to rejoin the Union. In his view, the eleven states of the Confederacy had been segregated from the mainstream of American life far too long. For much of this, he blamed the North. However, he also believed that the South had to take the lead in reconciliation—not because he thought it was guilty of anything but because, as a practical man, he did not think the North would take any real initiative. This conviction of his led to one of the most misunderstood incidents of his career—the Russell candidacy of 1952.

The announcement of his Presidential candidacy was widely misinterpreted in the press. It was obvious to even the dullest wit in the Senate Press Gallery that Russell was too intelligent a man to believe that he could win a nomination for the White House. Therefore, his campaign was treated as a tactic to gain concessions for the South in the Democratic Party platform and, possibly, to provide a means of delivering the Southern states to the Republican

Party. The candidacy was regarded as an ominous sign for the Democratic Party. In reality, it was one of the few good things that happened to the party that year.

The real objective was to prevent a Southern bolt from the Democratic Party. It was definitely in the cards. The Thurmond-Wright "States Rights" Party had failed to carry enough of the Southern states in the 1948 campaign to throw the election into the House of Representatives. But that was largely due to the left-wing character of the Wallace campaign, which actually drove many Southerners back into the regular Democratic camp. There was no such left-wing movement on the horizon in 1952 and it would have taken very little to organize a movement that would split the Democratic convention right down the middle. In Russell's eyes, such a split would cost the South valuable allies in the Democratic Party and leave Dixie to the tender mercies of the Republicans whom he did not expect to be grateful. There was no one else in a position to act and he stepped into the breach.

Even though the MacArthur hearings were far in the past, it was still taken for granted that I was to work with Russell on any national project. This meant that I sat in—with Lyndon B. Johnson—on the planning sessions of his Presidential candidacy in 1952. The announcement of the candidacy had two major objectives. First, it prevented anyone else from organizing a movement to lead a Southern revolt. The Russell name was magic anywhere below the Mason-Dixon line and no other hat would be tossed into the ring. Second, it paved the way for Russell to rise at the end of the convention to make the statement that had he won he would have expected the support of Northern Democrats and he could not have had such expectations unless he and his followers were prepared to support a Northern winner. All of the plans worked according to the forecast and even though the Democrats were unable to carry all the Southern states, the party at least avoided a convention split that could have been devastating.

There was one factor, however, upon which we had not counted. We could not present Russell as a serious national candidate unless he campaigned in the North. On one of his early trips to New Jersey, a Democratic political leader (probably thinking he was being kind) said: "We would like to support you, Senator. You're the best man. But we cannot support a Southerner." Variations on this theme cropped up in every Northern visit, leaving Russell a bitter man. He had known intellectually that the professionals of the North could not support a Southern candidate. But intellectual knowledge and gut knowledge are two different things. To the few friends who knew what had happened, he became a tragic figure.

Perhaps a more important offshoot of Russell's desire to put a final end to the Civil War was his conclusion that the process could be speeded by the election of a Southern President and that Lyndon B. Johnson was the only man from a Confederate state who stood a chance. He based his logic on two considerations. First, Johnson represented Texas and Russell was convinced that most Northerners thought of Texas as west rather than south. Second, Johnson's legislative record had ranged from moderate to liberal on a number of issues concerning public power. There was only one other Senator from a Confederate state who occupied a similar position. It was Estes Kefauver, who had so alienated his Southern colleagues that he was regarded as being totally outside the bloc.

Russell had no illusions about his project. He understood that no Senator with a record completely satisfactory to Georgia, Alabama, or Mississippi could be elected President. At the same time, however, he did not believe that anyone could alienate the South completely and achieve the office, either. Therefore, what was required was the walking of a tightrope that would create for Johnson an image of a national leader with a degree of acceptance in every part of the United States. It was an ambitious project and he recognized the difficulties. But he thought it was worth taking the risk.

As part of his design, he set out to buy Lyndon Johnson some elbowroom in dealing with the Southern bloc. His efforts had far-reaching consequences. With his colleagues, he argued that the election of a Southerner as President—even a very liberal Southerner—was the only course that gave the South an opportunity to expect decent treatment at the hands of the rest of the country. Day after day, he pounded home the assertion that civil rights legislation was ultimately inevitable and the only real option was whether it would be administered reasonably or unreasonably. Whether his plans actually led to Johnson's accession to the Vice Presidency and the Presidency, I do not know. But there is little doubt that they paved the way for passage of considerable legislation normally repugnant to the South during the eight years of Johnson's leadership.

There was one other major center of power in the Senate during those years. It was Robert A. Taft of Ohio, who had become known as "Mr. Republican." Looking back upon the period affords another lesson in the American political process. There was no better known Republican in the United States during most of his lifetime. Yet today, despite a massive stone monument to his memory at the foot of Capitol Hill, he is almost completely forgotten. When I mention his name in a gathering of relatively sophisticated people, most of them think I am referring to his father—a rather colorless President—or possibly to the sculptor Lorado Taft. We live in a country where only the Presidency is a sure ticket to political immortality.

During his lifetime, Taft was regarded as the focal point of opposition to Democratic Presidents. Reporters would rush directly to his office from Presidential press conferences to seek a comment. They were never disappointed. Frequently, the headlines on Presidential initiatives would couple his name with that of the White House occupant—so much so that I suspect many people believed him to be a part of the Truman administration. The press was right. The most important question to ask after a Presidential proposal was how Taft would react to it. His power in Congress could not be ignored.

Taft's power at Republican conventions, however, was an altogether different story. Twice he mounted major bids for the Republican nomination; twice the bid was defeated decisively. Outside of his native Ohio, he had no control over the nominating machinery. A substantial proportion of his delegates at both conventions where he was a contender came from the ex-Confederate states where the Republican Party was regarded as a joke— small bands of powerless hopefuls seeking to jump on the bandwagon of a winning nominee in hopes that they would be rewarded with some patronage.

The American political parties have peculiar characteristics that set them off from almost any other in the world. One, which has been noted by many commentators, is the division between the Presidential party and the Congressional party—a split that exists among both Democrats and Republicans. This split has consequences. It means that a sitting President will receive far less cooperation from his own party in Congress than he had anticipated. It also means that the Congressional branch of either party hogs the spotlight during years that the party does not occupy the White House. By 1952, the Republican Party had been excluded from the White House for twenty years. This meant that in the eyes of the public— or, at least, that part of the public that paid attention to government—the Republican Party *was* the Congressional party and that meant the party of Robert A. Taft.

As a working journalist, I covered Taft in Congress and at Republican conventions. The contrast was so extreme that there were times when I thought I was covering two different men. In the Senate, Taft was in command. He was decisive, knowledgeable, deft. He and Russell did not even have to meet to operate the Republican–Southern Democratic coalition. As Lyndon Johnson was to say later: "Bob Taft and Dick Russell ran this place with a wink and a nod." At Republican conventions, the kindest description of the man was bumbler. He had no grasp of the dynamics of convention politics and he assembled convention staffs that were completely incompetent. In the 1948 convention, Tom Dewey stole whole state delegations from under his nose and in 1952 he was made to look like a thief attempting to thwart the will of the people of Texas by foisting upon them a phony delegation. Both times, his performance was pitiful.

As soon as the conventions were over, however, he reverted to the Taft of power. General Eisenhower opened reconciliation negotiations with him almost immediately following the closing gavel. This was not just a question of amassing votes for the 1952 election. Ike realized that as President he would have to deal with Taft every day of the year. He could reach the White House without any help from the Ohioan. But he could not run the country without at least a nominal relationship of party harmony between the two men. The relationship was little more than that. The two dealt at arm's length and the coolness set up ideal conditions for the Congressional Democrats to play Eisenhower against his own party.

There were lesser powerhouses whose names have now been forgotten—men like Kerr of Oklahoma; Hayden of Arizona; Anderson of New Mexico; Johnson of Colorado. Any one of them could swing blocs of votes that meant life or death to a bill. What is interesting, however, is that none of them were very well known to the public even in their days of power. The spotlight was far more likely to swing to men who carried no weight in the legislative process other than their individual votes. These were the Presidential candidates. They illustrated the truism that even a bid for the Presidency will capture more popular attention than parliamentary skill.

Three of the men who served in the Senate during the 1950s did become President. They were Richard M. Nixon, John F. Kennedy, and Lyndon B. Johnson. Of that trio, however, only Johnson could reasonably be described as a major force in the legislative process. Nixon's reputation rested almost entirely on the communist investigations he had held in the House of Representatives.

Kennedy's reputation had far more to do with his social position than his only Congressional achievement: an investigation of labor racketeering. Both had high degrees of competency. But neither was very interested in Capitol Hill. They looked upon the Senate floor as a sounding board that would help them project their pleas for Executive power—the goal that really meant something to them. It was a question of temperament.

Next to Taft, the best-known Senator of that period was probably Estes Kefauver of Tennessee. His only legislative achievement had been an investigation of organized crime. But he had beaten a well-known political boss—Ed Crump of Memphis—during the period when bosses had become very unpopular and he had a superb sense of public relations.

There were other would-be Presidential candidates— such as Henry "Scoop" Jackson of Washington and Stu Symington of Missouri. They did not make much of an impact upon the Senate, despite considerable ability. One who did was Hubert Humphrey of Minnesota. He was a remarkable man who wound up possessing both legislative skill and the kind of public recognition that under other circumstances could have led him to the White House. Unfortunately for him, he received the Democratic nomination in 1968 after four years as Lyndon Johnson's Vice President. The opposition to the Vietnamese war had reached a fever pitch and no one associated with Johnson could possibly have won an election in that year. It was a miracle that Hubert came as close to winning as he did. He was nosed out by Nixon by less than a percentage point.

Were this a book entitled "Interesting Characters I

Have Met," this chapter could be continued indefinitely. But this is a book about the Senate as a whole. Those I have listed include the major components of the problems involved in running the Senate during the decade of the fifties. Their identification was essential for what follows to make sense. The difficulty that confronted Lyndon B. Johnson, when he assumed the Democratic leadership in 1953, was to break up some of the blocs (such as the Republican–Southern Democratic coalition) and put others together (such as the Western reclamation area states bloc and the labor blocs of the Northeast). I am too far from the Senate today to hazard more than a guess on its current composition. But I am confident that the basic problem remains the same—how to weld independent baronies into a unified force.

7
Building Unity

One of the oddities of American politics is the impact of a Presidential contest on the Congress. Victory has a tendency to fragment the legislative branch of either party; defeat has a tendency to unify it. This, in turn, means that once the famous Presidential "honeymoon" is over, the occupant of the oval office finds no automatic majorities in the House and the Senate that will put through his programs for him. Instead, he must go through the laborious process of patching up parliamentary coalitions to gain support for every project he sends to Capitol Hill. Frequently, he discovers that he cannot make any move successfully without concessions to Senators and Representatives that are nominally in opposition to him.

Sometimes the honeymoon is fairly lengthy. Franklin

D. Roosevelt, for example, *did* have automatic Democratic majorities for his first two years and had no worries about Republicans. When the process of Democratic fragmentation began to set in, he required a considerable amount of time to adjust to the realities. Eventually he did and what successes he had during his second and third terms—both in domestic and foreign policy—put him in debt heavily to Republicans such as Charles McNary of Oregon and Warren R. Austin of Vermont. Harry S Truman kicked his honeymoon away before his first term had ended, and his inability to negotiate with Republicans was a major factor in reducing him to a state of impotence. There was too strong a streak of partisanship in him to take advantage of warm friendships he had on the Republican side of the aisle.

As far as his own party was concerned, Eisenhower never had a honeymoon. The Democratic strategy of playing him off against the Republican Senators worked from the beginning. His period of peace and harmony with legislators was mostly on the Democratic side of the Senate aisle. There were a number of factors at work that made Ike a unifier of the Democrats but also a disrupter of Republican unity.

Generally speaking, it is far easier to hold a legislative wing of an American political party together when the party does not control the White House. Both the Senators and Representatives purge themselves of many of their combative instincts by taking out their aggressions on the President. Furthermore, they are a minority, most of the time, and the nature of the American political process is such that minorities tend to plot to capture the top spot and are held together by their desire to escape the minority tag. Members of a minority legislative faction will even go out of their way to smooth over differences in their ranks. The Republicans had been out of power for thirty years when Eisenhower took over the Presidency and during those three decades they had swept their differences under the rug, rather than resolving them.

The split between the Middle Western Republicans and their brothers on the two coasts was deep. The Progressive wing of the party, which had played such an important role in the twenties in the Prairie and North Central states, had fairly well disappeared. Its members had left the GOP to form such splinter parties as the Progressives in Wisconsin or the Farmer-Laborites in Minnesota and, when it became apparent that third parties do not flourish in the American system, had shifted even further to the Democratic Party. This left the conservatives in virtually complete control of the GOP from the Appalachians to the Rocky Mountains. Their bedrock was the farmer and the small businessman—tired of taxes, angry over social and economic regulations, and deeply suspicious of the "city slickers" who seemed to be in control of party affairs in the East and the West. Generally speaking, this was known as the "Taft wing" as opposed to the "Dewey wing"—named after the New York district attorney who was twice a Presidential candidate. The Taft wing controlled Congress, which meant that it was the public face of the party. But the Dewey wing controlled the convention machinery, which meant that it wound up naming all of the candidates. It was a situation bound to erupt in trouble.

During the thirty years of Democratic hegemony over the White House, the split was not too apparent. It surfaced every four years but went away again as soon as the election was over. But even though it was kept quiet, it grew in bitterness—especially where the Taft people were concerned. They felt that they were the only effective branch of the Republican Party and that every four years they were robbed by trickery of what should have been their rightful reward—naming the party's Presidential candidate. When Eisenhower won in 1952, they were not very happy. In their eyes, his nomination had been made possible only by fast footwork on the part of the Dewey machinery and they were not at all pleased with the prominence given to Dewey associates in the President's official family—such as Herbert Brownell as Attorney General and Jim Haggerty as White House Press Secretary.

The fears of the Taft wing were more than justified. Eisenhower gave them no comfort whatsoever on their cherished isolationism. And he did not start to dismantle the New Deal—the long dream of the Middle Western GOP. He made it quite clear to them that he had no great problem with FDR's social legislation except that he wanted to cut it back to a more sensible pace.

With such a background, Eisenhower's clashes with the Senate Republicans were inevitable. Even though, as I remarked previously, the doctrines of isolation were not embraced by all Republicans, almost all of the isolationists had joined the Republican Party. This made the House of Representatives and the Senate the last bastions of the idea that the United States should refuse to participate in world affairs except at arm's length. As the final years of the Roosevelt administration had been dominated by issues of international concern, the isolationists associated their concepts with opposition to the New Deal. This was not too much of a problem in the House of Representatives, where the large Republican delegations from the Eastern Seaboard were in reasonably good control. But the Senate GOP was largely controlled by men from the Middle West who were opposed to what they called "entangling alliances" with other nations and who hated FDR with an intensity that had to be seen at close range to be credited.

The situation was made to order for a man like Lyndon Johnson. He had some firm principles, most of which ran along the lines of agrarian populism. But he was always willing to take half a loaf when he could not get the full one. And one of his principles was, held with a zeal I regarded as somewhat excessive, a deep conviction that Congress should not get in the way of the President in the field of foreign policy. In short, he was willing to "make a deal" and as far as he and the President were concerned, all of the necessary ingredients were present. Finally, although he was not deep in terms of goals and substantive thought, he was fantastically subtle when it came to getting things done. Once he knew where he should be headed, he could always find a way of persuading a majority to go where he wanted it to go.

The Eisenhower victory in 1952 resulted in a unification of the Senate Democrats almost as quickly as it led to fragmentation of the Republicans. Part of this was due to salesmanship by Lyndon B. Johnson. He spent hour after hour in personal conferences with the Democrats, bombarding them with arguments on the advantages of supporting Ike against the Republicans. His arguments were simple but effective. In the first place, he pointed out to them, it was a strategy that was totally anti-Republican but avoided the uncertain business of fighting an American hero. In the second place, he argued, it made the Republicans look cheap and partisan, whereas the Democrats would resemble statesmen willing to put petty issues of partisanship aside to battle for the public good. Finally, he pointed out, Ike was not going to be running for another four years anyway and this meant that the political concentration should be on defeating Republicans in the senatorial elections of 1954. Should 1956—the next Presidential year—call for a different strategy, there was plenty of time to reconsider and adopt it.

There were a few Democrats who were unhappy with the strategy. They had adopted the philosophy that it was "the business of the opposition to oppose"—a principle that had first been stated by Taft. But on foreign policy considerations they were in no position to oppose Eisenhower, anyway. And on domestic policy considerations, they could not really do very much harm. Even these few Democrats withdrew their opposition to Johnson when the 1954 elections returned Democratic majorities to both legislative branches. It is one thing to argue against a theory; a different thing to argue against success.

At the fine arts of persuasion, Johnson was always an effective man. But his cajolery would not have worked had it not been for another development—the demise of the Republican–Southern Democratic coalition. Very few people had realized that the Republican victory would mean an end to this unnatural alliance. Some observers in the press had even made the mistake of assuming that it would continue with Johnson as a stooge for Russell. They had missed the fact that the combination had utility only as long as a Democratic President occupied the White House.

The major motivation for the alliance had been to block civil rights legislation, toward which Republicans were generally quite neutral (there were a few exceptions who passionately advocated integration but these were too few to matter). What they had done was to acquiesce in the arrangement in exchange for Southern Democratic help in killing economic bills that they opposed. On most of these bills, they could rely on a Republican President to exercise a veto. Therefore, the coalition no longer seemed to them a basic necessity. At the same time, the presence of a Republican in the White House relaxed to a minor, but still important, degree the apprehensions of the Southern bloc. This was because they were not quite as afraid of an integration law signed by a Republican as they were one signed by a Democratic President. They had many reasons at that point for wanting to keep the Democratic Party intact in the South, and a Democratic Presidential signature on a civil rights bill would have created political chaos. A Republican Presidential signature would not lure local Southern leaders into turning Republican.

There was still another reason contributing to the formation of Democratic unity. It was Richard Russell's campaign to make Lyndon B. Johnson President. It was a highly successful campaign but, like almost everything else in the real world, it was not just a question of logic and persuasion. Forces were at work that made the Southerners more than ready to accept the Russell arguments. These forces illustrate the basic realities of Senate life so well that a complete analysis deserves a separate chapter. For the time being, all that need be noted is that it worked and that it gave Johnson an enormous advantage.

Actually, the success of the Russell campaign enabled Johnson to swing much further to the left than would have been possible for any Northern Democrat seeking to hold the party together. He had the best of all possible worlds for a Senate leader. He was specifically exempted from Southern attacks. He was not required to take part in such Dixie maneuvers as "The Southern Manifesto," a rather forlorn document signed by the other Confederate state Senators reaffirming the so-called states' rights (actually anti-integration) cause. And whenever they could do so without harming their home base, his Southern colleagues would engage in elaborate maneuvers that would assure his success as a leader of liberal proposals, which they opposed. One example is well worth recording here as it not only demonstrates the extent of the immunity LBJ enjoyed from the South but also gives some picture of what can be maneuvered in a parliamentary body when sufficient will exists.

In 1956, Eisenhower sent the Congress a Presidential message proposing a housing bill that, among other things, included authority to construct 35,000 public housing units. This was a period in which both Middle Western Republicans and Southern Democrats were staunchly opposed to public housing, which they regarded as a direct form of socialism. The number 35,000 had probably been selected by the President on the basis of advice that this was the most attainable and that to get even that figure would require the use of all his prestige. It should be noted here that the measure carried many other provisions involving mortgage financing that were universally popular.

By a weird quirk, the Senate Banking and Currency Committee, which had jurisdiction over housing measures, was heavily stacked with housing liberals. They promptly upped the 35,000 public housing units to 750,000 and sent the bill to the floor, where it was obvious that a majority would be in opposition to that particular provision. The Senate Republicans scented victory and Senator Homer Capehart of Indiana prepared an amendment to cut the public units back to the Eisenhower request. It was taken for granted that his amendment would prevail. No one thought it would be possible to muster enough votes to override the Republicans and Southern Democrats who regarded public housing as socialism.

A word of explanation as to Senate procedure is necessary here. The 750,000 units were already in the bill because of the action of the committee. This meant that a yea vote on the Capehart amendment would eliminate the provision and return things to the Eisenhower figure. A nay vote, on the other hand, was a positive affirmation of the provision for 750,000 units. This was entirely clear to anyone familiar with Senate procedure. It was *not* so clear, however, to people unaccustomed to parliamentary matters. Most of us live in a world where yea is yea and nay is nay. It is only in Congress that yea can be nay and nay can be yea.

One of the advantages of dealing with the Southern bloc in those days was that its members knew how to reach complete and binding agreement without any word of their intentions leaking to the outside. The Southern Senators delivered the customary number of anti–public housing speeches on the Senate floor and both the Republicans and the press thought that they were foreshadowing the vote on the anti–public housing amendment. Capehart even went so far as to twit Johnson on his forthcoming defeat minutes before the vote. Johnson had already achieved something of a reputation as a miracle worker but there was a consensus that this time the magic could not come through.

The first Southern name on the roll call was Harry Flood Byrd of Virginia. He was not only a Southern Democrat. He was probably the most conservative member in either party of the Senate. He was as far to the right as a man could be and still remain in the bounds of sanity. There was no one who hated "socialism" as much as Byrd. When he voted "nay" in a clear, ringing voice on the amendment, Capehart's head jerked around so rapidly I was afraid his neck was going to snap. For once, it was the literal truth to say that a man's jaw dropped as Southerner after Southerner voted against the Capehart amendment. It was defeated overwhelmingly and the Senate went on record for 750,000 public housing units. It was not the most important Lyndon Johnson triumph in his eight years as Senate leader. But it was the most stunning upset that he had maneuvered in his career.

I do not know whether anybody ever explained to Capehart what had happened. The Southern Democrats left the floor as soon as the vote was announced and hastened to the Senate recording facilities where they had themselves plugged in to radio stations all over their home states. There they explained to their constituents that they had voted against the Capehart amendment because it still represented socialism—35,000 units of it. They produced masterpieces of improvisation. Socialism, in their view, was not a question of quantity but of quality. Some of them even lambasted as "left wingers" the conservative Republicans who had supported Capehart. To anyone who understood Senate procedures, their arguments could be described only in the immortal words of Winston Churchill—"thinner than soup made by boiling the shadow of a pigeon." Like so many other things, however, Senate procedures are thoroughly understood only in the Senate.

There were two factors that lent verisimilitude to the Southern stand. The first, I have mentioned already. It was the seemingly *negative* character of the vote affirming the 750,000 units. All that many of the Senators had to say was: "I voted no against socialistic public housing." After all, it *had* been a nay vote and many constituents looked no further. The clincher, however, was that the Southerners then told their people that they were going to vote against the whole bill because of the public housing provision. This was a perfectly safe vote because the Republicans who had pushed the Capehart amendment did not dare vote against the mortgage financing provisions. I should add, incidentally, that in the conference committee between the Senate and the House of Representatives, the 750,000 units were promptly scaled down. So the net effect of all the maneuvering was that the Southern bloc deliberately handed Johnson a legislative triumph that attracted attention all over the nation; presented the act to Southern voters as one of striking a blow against socialism; and finally wound up without an excess of housing units anyway. Merlin the magician could have done no better.

To this day, I am not certain whether Johnson was really contemplating a bid for the Presidency during the Senate years. The man was a master at concealing his motives even from himself. It is difficult to believe that a man of his driving ambition would not want to occupy the top spot. On the other hand, once he had mastered the Senate leadership, life started to become somewhat pale. The "middle years" syndrome, so familiar to psychologists, assailed him with doubts that political power was worth it. At times, he threatened to chuck the whole thing and go back to Austin. I myself believe that he was torn in two directions.

Whatever his inner motives, however, there can be no doubt that the Presidency campaign was useful to him. Without it, he could not have become the master of the Senate that he did. The Southern Democrats would have abandoned the alliance with the Republicans under any circumstances. But it would have been a slow, drawn-out enterprise. Furthermore, at that particular time no other Southern Senator could possibly have taken Johnson's place. The only other man from a Confederate state that could have been regarded as Presidential timber was Estes Kefauver of Tennessee. His state as a whole was not very Southern and he was even less so.

The basic point, however, is that when Johnson took over the Senate Democratic leadership in 1952, everything was working in his favor. A Republican President in the White House brought out strains in the Republican party that had been muted as long as its members could be united against a Democratic Chief Executive. The major Eisenhower interest in government was in the field of foreign policy, where he was actually more at home with the Democrats than with the Republicans. At the same time, the Democrats were finding an end to the forces that had kept them apart. They no longer had to worry about a Democratic President stirring up trouble with their constituents. And the Southern wing of the Democratic Party found itself with what it regarded as an overriding motive for reaching an accord with their Northern colleagues—a possible Southern President. What Johnson was really confronting was a "piece of cake." Nothing was required for his success except hard work—which he was always willing to do—and keeping his head—which Russell was willing to do for him.

8

The Coalition
Under a
Microscope

The history of the Republican–Southern Democratic coalition needs a more careful analysis than it has been given up to this point. We have been treating it solely in terms of the possibilities for unification that its demise opened up in the Senate. It is also worth looking at from the standpoint of the manner in which the Senate operates. Fundamentally, that is a question of the constant formation of new blocs and the dissolution of the older ones as the reasons for their existence disappears. It is rare for any of the combinations to have any degree of permanence, and those that last beyond two or three years are exceptional.

The Republican–Southern Democratic alliance was an exception. It lasted well over a decade. And, unlike the other coalitions, it governed the options open to the

Southern members over a wide range of subjects. As a rule, a Senate alliance restricts the action that may be taken by the participants only on the specific issues involved. The Dixie Senators, however, were at the mercy of the conservative Republicans upon virtually every social issue that could appear on the legislative calendar. Their absolute need to prevent civil rights legislation from reaching the floor had led them into a one-sided deal.

The coalition was a creation of the mid-thirties. Prior to that, it had not been necessary. The handful of Senators truly interested in civil rights were motivated solely by idealism. It is an invariable rule of legislative activity that measures are passed because of constituent pressures. Idealism serves only to keep the concepts alive until the stronger motives compel action. As a footnote, this is one of the reasons why the first stirrings on civil rights legislation were in the House of Representatives. In the 1920s and early 1930s, black Americans had become sufficiently well integrated into urban districts to bring pressure to bear on House members. It was not until the late thirties that Senators, who have broader constituencies, began to feel the heat.

In the early days of the New Deal, Franklin Delano Roosevelt relied heavily upon the Southern Senators to push his programs through the chamber. These included men from the very heart of Dixie—such as Pat Harrison of Mississippi and James Byrnes from South Carolina—as well as the border states, whose New Dealers were Joe Robinson from Arkansas and Kenneth McKellar from Tennessee. Their Populist backgrounds fit perfectly into the social uplift wave pushed by FDR. Reporters covering the U.S. Senate in the thirties actually relied upon Byrnes to tell them when the White House would or would not accept changes in legislation.

As time went on, however, the civil rights issue came increasingly to the fore. A slow, but perceptible, shift got under way and the face of the South in the Senate began to resemble "Cotton Ed" Smith, also from South Carolina, who campaigned openly on racial bigotry. The shift was hastened by Roosevelt's selection of Smith and Senator Walter F. George of Georgia as two of his prime targets in the 1938 "purge campaign," where he sought to bring about the selection of Democratic candidates who would go along with him. The campaign was virtually a complete failure (Tammany managed to redistrict out of his seat a New York Representative whom Roosevelt disliked) but it left bitter emotions in its wake. There were Southerners who normally would have confined their anti-FDR feelings to civil rights legislation only but who came to hate him clear across the board. Incidentally, it should be added that the purge campaign had nothing to do with civil rights. It was retaliation for opposition to the New Deal Supreme Court reorganization bill.

The formation of the coalition seemed quite natural at the time it took place. The Southerners—even those who were pro–New Deal—felt no particular loyalty to the Democratic Party. To them, the Democratic label was merely a device to prevent blacks from being effective at the polls (in the event that any of them were able to master the other barriers that blocked access to the franchise). They operated on the legal theory that the party was a private club that was not covered by the Constitutional guarantees on the right to vote. Once the whites had selected their own candidates, it was no great feat to convert the general election in November into a perfunctory endorsement of the lily-white Democratic primaries that had taken place earlier.

The Republican parties in the South presented no threat to the Democratic state and county courthouse Democratic machines. There were only three ex-Confederate states that had Republican organizations of any substantial size. They were Texas, where the GOP was an ethnic group of the descendants of the German settlers who came to the United States in the mid-nineteenth century; North Carolina, where outrageous gerrymandering had crammed virtually all Republicans into one district in the Piedmont; and Tennessee, whose eastern districts were solidly Republican but whose western areas, where most of the people lived, were solidly Democratic. In addition, there were minuscule clusters of Republicans throughout Appalachia. Nowhere, however, could they make a real impact upon Southern life. Those who adhered to the party of Abraham Lincoln were freaks who could expect no reward for their activity other than a few crumbs of patronage if their delegates hopped aboard the right bandwagon at a national convention. At the time, it seemed to me that there was real significance to the fact that these delegates were basic to the convention strength of Robert A. Taft during his two bids for the Presidency. He could not draw in the Northern states, outside of Ohio, where his party was a vital force. It was a poor base for an assault on the White House.

At no time had the Southern Democrats shared the loyalties of their Northern colleagues toward their party. They were Democrats only because of historical accident that had dumped the anti-slavery cause into the pockets of the Republican Party. Furthermore, from the end of Reconstruction in 1875 to the mid-thirties, the GOP had been basically the party of industrialization, high tariffs, and high interest rates—concerns that ran contrary to the interests of the agricultural Southland. During the same period, the Northern base of the Democratic Party had been the big-city machines, which were indifferent to Southern institutions, including segregation. There were heavy strains in the 1920s over such issues as the Ku Klux Klan and prohibition of alcoholic beverages, which led many Southerners to vote Republican in 1928 against Al Smith, a Democratic Catholic candidate for the Presidency. But these battles, however fierce, did not make any impact upon Congressional Democrats. They were another illustration of the differences between America's Presidential and legislative parties.

The 1932 election was overshadowed by the Great Depression—a problem that suspended all other issues and put antagonisms on back burners. In retrospect, Franklin D. Roosevelt was elected President on the basis of one mandate—"Do something! Anything!" None were very certain what they wanted done nor did they care as long as it put people back to work or at least on a payroll. Roosevelt responded in the same spirit. He did something and he did everything. Whether the New Deal could claim responsibility for restoring the economy is a moot question. But the mere fact of activity was heartening. In the Senate of the United States, FDR supporters from the South were still with him even after the desertion of some Northern machine politicians and intellectuals such as Jim Farley from New York, his colleague Al Smith (who had been a close associate of FDR during their days in state politics), and Raymond Moley, an original member of the brain trust. Although Roosevelt could not be accurately termed a "Populist," there was enough of a Populist strain in his policies to capture the allegiance of the Southerners.

There was another force at work, however, It was the rising political strength of the blacks. Displaced from the plantations by the Rust cotton picker and newly invented cultivating machines, they had crowded into big cities— an environment in which reasonably substantial minorities can become effective politically in a relatively short time. They were living together where they could talk over their grievances and plan action. At the same time, their massed numbers gave them protection against white retaliation for voting. Originally, they voted Republican because they thought of the party in terms of Abraham Lincoln. The first black Congressman from Chicago, for example, was Oscar DePriest, a member of the GOP. But in a few years, they heard a sympathetic voice in the White House itself—Mrs. Franklin D. Roosevelt. It would be an oversimplification to say that she led them into the Democratic Party. The Northern Democratic city machines were primarily Irish who would move over and make room for any group that was having a substantial impact on urban politics. But Mrs. Roosevelt gave the blacks the feeling that the Democratic Party was on "our side" and their shift in allegiance as a result had many implications.

In the days of the city machines, power in a city led ultimately to a degree of power in the nation. The city bosses survived by obliging their constituent blocs and if one of those blocs needed something from the federal government, the city bosses knew how to exercise the kind of influence that would secure a response. This was particularly true in the early days of the New Deal when Franklin Delano Roosevelt relied heavily upon Hague of Jersey City; Kelly-McCloskey of Philadelphia; Kelly of Chicago; and the various New York City organizations, including Tammany, to deliver key states in an election. These men, of course, did not become pro-integrationists. But they created in their states an atmosphere of "dealing" with the blacks that was bound to have echoes in Washington. What was even more important, however, was that Northern Democratic Senators were heavily dependent upon big majorities in the metropolitan areas to offset the largely Republican rural vote. This meant that civil rights was graduating from a cause of conscience to a cause of constituency. The constituency was Democratic.

The black migration to the big cities did not have the same impact upon Congressional Republicans in the North. Their political base was in the rural areas and the suburbs. They did not need the huge urban vote that was a "must" for any successful senatorial Democrat from such states as New York, Pennsylvania, Illinois, or Ohio. Of course, there were individual Republicans who supported civil rights legislation out of conscience. But this was not a question of constituent pressures. From the standpoint of getting elected, they could afford to play it cool. This was the reason why they were the dominant factor in the Republican–Southern Democratic coalition. They could go either way with impunity.

There was one other group that could "swing" at any time and in any manner that it wished. This included the Senators from the Rocky Mountain states who, in those days, were largely Democratic. Civil rights was an issue remote from their constituencies. They were perfectly willing to vote for an integration bill should it ever appear on the floor of the Senate. They were equally willing to cooperate in keeping the bill within a committee or preventing the imposition of cloture during debate. It depended on the situation. The earlier settlers of their states had, to a great extent, been migrants from the Confederacy after the Civil War. Consequently, they had some slight sympathies for the Southern opposition to integration. But the sympathies were very slight and when a civil rights bill finally surfaced in 1957, they played a vital role in assisting it to passage. In the early part of the decade, however, they were something of an obstacle to integration measures.

The most important factor, however, was probably the industrialization of the South. It was a development that was greeted with glee in Dixie, as it meant payrolls and new money to a region that was suffering heavily from a narrow allegiance to basic agriculture. Whole areas of the South were dependent upon single commodities—cotton, tobacco, rice, citrus—and if anything went wrong with one of those commodities, the region suffered. World War II had brought about some drastic changes in world markets and most of them worked against the South. Mainland China, for example, was the major outlet for Texas cotton (Texas was the largest single producer of that crop) and this market was lost completely in the chaos that followed the Japanese surrender. Furthermore, England, which had taken so much of the tobacco (and the extra-long staple cotton) along the Eastern Seaboard, had been compelled to shift to other sources.

The Old South, of course, was not completely devoid of

manufacturing. Birmingham, Alabama, had been in the business of making steel for many decades. There were shipyards along both the Atlantic Coast and the Gulf of Mexico. The Carolinas had begun to lure the textile mill owners of New England long before World War II. But there was no state that could be termed "industrial" in the sense that one would use the word for Connecticut or New Jersey, and the manufacturing areas were not political factors of prime importance. Southern politics was dominated by a rural mentality, even in the large cities. It was totally unprepared for the impact of industrialization.

As they are discovering in South Africa today, capitalism and segregation do not get along well together. It is not at all difficult, ignoring for the moment the moral question, to keep races apart in a plantation economy. The group that has been assigned a status of inferiority can be compelled to live in shacks on the plantation itself. They can be required to draw their supplies from a single source and their hours of work can be set by an overseer who can escort them out to the fields in the morning and back to their huts in the evening. It is a miserable, mean-spirited way of life and its economic validity is dubious. But it can be made to work without too great an expenditure of coercive power.

An industrialized society, on the other hand, assumes that workers are free agents. It may not treat them very well. But it leaves them free to shift from job to job and it lays upon the employee, rather than an overseer, the responsibility of getting to work on time and doing the job properly. Of course, the worker gets fired if he or she doesn't perform to standard but this is regarded as one of the normal rules of the game. The capitalist seeks a free labor market where he or she has few responsibilities of custodial care for the people who man his or her plants. The union movement has prevented this freedom from being absolute but it still exists. Even the most favorable labor-management contract permits management hiring and firing of workers.

In the early days of Southern industrialization, segregation could be maintained merely by hiring white workers for the favored jobs and restricting the blacks to the messier forms of maintenance. Even that, however, made some dent in segregation patterns. Industrialists had cost accountants who could give them some accurate figures on the expenses of racism. Some of them were interesting. The laws in the Southern states required separate toilets for blacks and whites. This meant that a manufacturer who was planning to hire some blacks had to invest extra money in plumbing and, if both men and women were involved, the cost could be very high.

As industrialization advanced, the problems of segregation became even more complicated. In the early 1960s, I was in contact with a manufacturer who was preparing to launch a major operation in the northern half of a Deep South state. He had surveyed his work force needs with great care and had concluded that the racial composition in the area was such that he could be successful only by employing large numbers of blacks from the local community. The next step in his chain of reasoning was that he wanted the ablest blacks in the area and could be sure of getting them only if he had a black assistant personnel manager. Here he ran into a stone wall. Men and women of the caliber he was seeking simply would not go to a Southern town where they could not try on clothing in a department store or where their children could not use the public parks or the swimming pools. The result of all this was that the manufacturer became the leading advocate of integration in the community, and he had the economic power to make it stick.

Obviously, none of this happened overnight. The integration of the South was not smooth at any point. There were confrontations; riots; and bloodied heads. But these were the death throes of a dying way of life and there were significant shifts in the cloakroom conversations of the Senate Democrats. The most important was that they were beginning to see the civil rights issue as a constituent necessity of their Northern colleagues and their alliance with the Republicans as a costly burden. None of this was expressed openly. It came out in little bits and snatches—straws in the wind—and one had to be thoroughly steeped in the ways of the Senate to realize what was happening.

For example, I have a vivid recollection of walking down a street in New York City with Senator John C. Stennis of Mississippi. We were holding some committee hearings, and during the lunch hour, we went through the teeming masses of the garment district to reach a restaurant. Stennis watched the flow of humanity and suddenly turned to me and said: "George, if I lived here, I would be for every bit of that civil rights legislation." That may not sound like an important statement. But it must be remembered that the Southern Senators had based their filibuster tactics on the assumption that nobody really wanted civil rights except a few crackpots. As long as they could cling firmly to this belief, they had no moral scruples against talking integration bills to death without permitting them to come to a vote. The discovery that there

were strong constituent pressures would not alter their opposition to civil rights. But it was bound to shake the
moral base that had enabled them to prevent a serious discussion of the issue.

There was another unforeseen aspect of industrialization that had a direct bearing on Southern politics. The
growth of manufacturing not only brought payrolls to the
South. It also brought a genuine Republican Party with
political organizations that could go out and challenge
Democrats for control of local offices. The Southern GOP
was no longer a collection of freaks. It was an organization
making a serious bid in every state.

The resurgence of the Republican Party first became
apparent in Texas. The petrochemical industry along the
gulf coast had become a giant. Northern management
methods and Northern managers had been introduced
and along with them came Northern Republicanism. Furthermore, the millionaires who were being made overnight wanted to hobnob with their fellow millionaires in
the Northeast and most of them were Republican. This
meant that the young, ambitious executives in their companies had Republican role models. In a matter of a few
years, what had been an ethnic party became a vibrant
factor in the state.

The transition sprang upon an unsuspecting public in
1952. Texas then had a system for selecting national convention delegations that virtually assured the triumph of
any well-organized majority. It began with party conventions in the 5,000 precincts of the state and, of course,
those conventions were rarely attended by many people.
They were advertised in a perfunctory manner but only
highly politicized and organized men and women would

even bother to find out where they were. The precinct conventions elected delegates to county conventions, which, in turn, elected delegates to the state convention. At the state convention, the delegates to the national convention were selected and given instructions on how to proceed. Obviously, the outcome was determined in the precincts.

For many years, this process had placed the Republican machinery in the hands of the ethnic Germans (known as Die Lands-leute) and their allies. In 1952, they favored Taft and it was generally thought that the Texas delegation would support the Ohio Senator. To everyone's amazement, however, there was a tidal wave of pro-Eisenhower voters that swept into the precinct conventions and took them away from the regulars. The Texas Republican State Committee refused to accept the results of the precinct conventions on the grounds that the Eisenhower supporters were interlopers. They selected their own pro-Taft delegation and the two separate groups showed up at the national convention to battle things out. Eisenhower won. But the more important aspect is that the controversy signaled the emergence of a real Republican Party in Texas. It did not take very long for other states to follow the Texas lead.

What this did was to make the Republican–Southern Democratic alliance in the Senate less attractive to both parties. The Republicans, for the first time since Reconstruction, saw a possibility of swelling their ranks from Dixie. The Democrats, for the first time since Reconstruction, saw the possibility of their local machines going down the drain. The more excruciating problem was the one presented to the Democrats.

Achievement in the Senate requires the formation of blocs. There are very few issues that can command voting majorities in and of themselves. Bills become law because of delicate trades; the snipping off of a piece here and the addition of a piece there; subtle compromises in which the favors that are done for some parties also load those parties with obligations. There are some Senators who do not play the game—who treat the Senate as a sounding board for advancing their views. Their position is entirely legitimate. They keep causes alive that otherwise would die. But they rarely do anything. Accomplishment eventually gets back to the members of the famous "club," which means the members that horse-trade.

In the Senate, the unforgivable sin is to ignore the constituency pressures of other Senators. No Senator is required to vote to solve the problems of another Senator or even to stand aside and aid in their solution. But to throw up barriers to legitimate consideration of those problems is to stand outside the pale. One can oppose but not smother. Ultimately, intransigence in preventing constituent issues from getting some form of action means isolation and isolation means ineffectiveness.

There are some Senators who either choose isolation deliberately or who play lone hands because they never become sufficiently aware of the workings of the Senate machinery. Generally speaking, these are the far-left liberals or the far-right conservatives who think of their political mission as evangelical. Their basic role is a search for converts to a cause and they have little interest in halfway measures. This is not a role to be despised. A Senate composed solely of "doers" would be a stodgy institution indeed. It is a body that requires the constant spur of the "true believers."

With very minor exceptions, the Southern Senators were not in that group. They wanted things done—things that would benefit their states. Consequently, with a few exceptions, they fell into the category defined by Lyndon B. Johnson as "workhorses" (as opposed to "showhorses"). In the early fifties, they were on the verge of deep trouble. Their Western state allies were not very reliable and their alliance with the Republicans was under heavy strain. They could not continue their opposition to *consideration* of civil rights legislation without accelerating the isolation process. At the same time, they could not openly toss in the sponge on civil rights without facing certain defeat at home. It was an excruciating dilemma.

These were the circumstances that made Richard Russell's Johnson-for-President campaign so attractive. Most Southern Senators were aware of the obvious fact that civil rights legislation was inevitable. The real issue was not whether such bills would be passed but whether there would be some obeisances made to the sensibilities of Southern whites. They could allow some things to "happen" (as they allowed the 1957 Civil Rights Act to pass without a filibuster) on the plea that they could not go too far in hamstringing a Southern Senate leader who might be President. At the same time, they were not required to make any public display of support for a Lyndon Johnson candidacy. The Russell strategy was to make Johnson look like a *national* leader and premature declarations would work against that goal. The Southerners were quite capable of discussing and laying elaborate plans without anything leaking to the outside world and that is precisely what they did.

The overall impact of all these considerations was that a bloc of twenty-two Senators was preparing to reenter the normal give-and-take of Senate politics at the very time Johnson took over the leadership. For at least a decade, they had been outside the customary process. Their role had been that of a bloc nominally within the Democratic Party but pitted against their fellow Democrats in the Senate on all domestic issues. Johnson, of course, was required to proceed carefully and to explore every step before taking it. But the surprise of the press when it was finally discovered that he was an effective leader was due to the failure of the press to understand the Republican–Southern Democratic coalition and the factors that were bringing it to an end. Johnson became a national political figure because he understood the forces at work.

9

Lines of
Strategy Form

When Lyndon Johnson assumed the floor leadership of the Democrats, the preconditions for unity were already in place. That, however, did not mean that unity was in place or would even follow automatically. The Northern wing of the Democratic Party blamed the Southerners for the Eisenhower victory and the Southern wing regarded the Northerners as "troublemakers" for being so persistent on the issue of civil rights. In addition, many of the more liberal Senators adopted what had once been the rallying cry of the Republican right wing under Democratic Presidents—"The business of the opposition is to oppose." This made absolutely no sense to the Dixie Democrats or their Western counterparts. They regarded their primary business as securing laws and federal projects to benefit their home states and could not see how opposition to a popular President would help them achieve that goal.

This division had an interesting base. There was a tendency on the part of industrial state Senators to put the capture of the White House ahead of the problems of their individual states. Many of them, in fact, regarded the Senate as a springboard for the Presidency, the job that really interested them. The Southern and Western Senators, on the other hand, had little or no chance of getting a serious nomination for the Presidency, and they knew it. In their universe, the highest conceivable goals of politics were the governor's mansion or the United States Senate. Consequently, they would go to extreme lengths to keep the people in their states happy.

The Johnson strategy of pitting the Senate Republicans against the President suited the Southerners and Westerners perfectly. First, it did not interfere with their search for goodies to send to their home states. Second, it kept things calm for a period of time so they could get some reading on the reactions of their constituents. Third, they felt a blessed sense of relief at not having to go home and explain why a Democratic President was doing so many things they did not like. They also knew that supporting the President on the issues he really felt strongly about, notably foreign policy, placed him in a position where he could not avoid reciprocity. Any time he wanted to pay off political debts, they were ready with suggestions for him as to how he could do it.

There was a different story with the Northern liberals. They were thinking in 1953 of running someone against Eisenhower in 1956 and they were looking for some ammunition to throw at the President. They wanted to fight and they were not easy to put off.

Fortunately, the answer to the liberals came in President Eisenhower's early appointments. The Republicans had been out of Executive power for so many years—twenty, to be exact—that they had lost the touch of government. The White House did not check its appointees with sufficient care and the omission handed the Democrats an issue on a silver platter. The first was the nomination of Charles Wilson as Secretary of Defense. He had resigned as head of General Motors to accept the cabinet post and had taken with him some very valuable GM stock options. General Motors was one of the largest suppliers to the Defense Department and the members of the Senate Armed Services Committee took exception. This led Mr. Wilson to a belligerency that was the biggest mistake of his life. He had the businessman's attitude toward politicians and regarded Senators as slightly below the rank of precinct captain. He saw no reason to dispose of his stock options in General Motors, because he was an honest man and, anyway, "What is good for the United States is good for General Motors and vice versa." It was a closed hearing and Democrats emerging from the session changed the quote slightly to: "What is good for General Motors is good for the United States and vice versa." The printed transcript corrected the quote for the record but not in the public mind. Mr. Wilson was promptly branded as the man who thought that serving General Motors was serving the United States. His nomination was not approved until he had sold all of his stock options at a heavy loss. It was a chastening experience for him and a shot in the arm for the liberal Democrats. It was a taste of the "red meat" for which they longed.

A lesser-known, but more important, controversy involved the nomination of a man named Lloyd Beeson to the National Labor Relations Board. He was known for his conservatism and liberal Democrats opened fire upon him immediately. They struck no responsive chord in their Southern colleagues. Even those who were pro-union in their outlook took the position that philosophy—unless it was outrageous—was no basis for turning down a Presidential nomination. The situation came to a head in a meeting of the Senate Democratic Policy Committee. As chairman, Johnson pointed out that during the hearings on his nomination Beeson had made important misstatements of fact concerning his financial position. Russell volunteered the statement that if three such instances could be documented, he would be inclined to vote no. It was an olive branch to his Northern colleagues. Within hours, a document circulated among the Senators supplying the facts. (A Dixie Senator who read it noted that this material was not in the official committee report and asked me whether it was "the Southern Supplement.") For the first time in years, there was a virtually unanimous Democratic vote on a substantive issue. The nomination was approved on the basis of Republican votes and when the term expired a year later it was not renewed.

The Beeson controversy was of prime significance to Lyndon B. Johnson. It enabled the liberals to take an anti-Eisenhower stance. It established his reputation as a leader of all the Senate Democrats rather than merely the head of a faction. It also offered an example of effectiveness after more than a decade of ineffective Democratic leadership. Most important, however, it demonstrated the validity of a strategy that was to work over and over again in the eight years ahead. It was to set up the issues in such a way as to enable all Democrats to vote together, while dividing the Republicans. In this particular instance, it had meant shifting the focus from Beeson's philosophy to Beeson's integrity. The shift had to be made after the nomination had been reported by the committee. After that, Johnson carried the principle one step further and went to work on the committees themselves.

Over the years of the Johnson leadership, reams of newspaper copy speculated on the LBJ magic. Very little of the speculation was valid. Stories were written on "arm twisting" and "log rolling" but the reality eluded the scribes. What was really happening was a tremendous effort that involved constant work with not only the committees but the committee staffs. Our staff—the Senate Democratic Policy Committee—worked with all of them and often could tell Johnson what would be in legislative committee reports before they were even put on paper. Johnson personally built up relations with staff members and kept a constant check on the attitudes of key Senators on bills that would come before them. It was delicate work as Senators are always supersensitive about their prerogatives and could be offended easily by "interference" in their domains.

I had covered the Senate as a newspaperman for many years. But it was during this period that I really learned how it operated. It was a revelation to me. The most important lesson was that virtually nothing would be done without rigid adherence to protocol; but that once protocol forms had been observed business could proceed with an ease and informality that have no parallels in any other field of endeavor. Two examples will make my point.

At the beginning of the fifties, the ranking Democrat on

the Senate Finance Committee, which handled taxes and tariffs, was Harry F. Byrd of Virginia. On economic matters, Byrd was the ultimate conservative—so much so that he was totally out of step with the committee and with the Senate. Even today he would be too far to the right. The effective control on the Democratic side was in the hands of relatively low-ranking Senators, such as Kerr of Oklahoma and Long of Louisiana. I have already mentioned another committee, which I shall not name, whose chairman had literally become senile. Again, the effective control was in the hands of a Democrat fairly far down the line. During my college days and thereafter, I had been nurtured on the concept of the absolute power of the committee chairmen. When I first learned of the situation involving these two committees, I was absolutely appalled.

It did not take me very long to discover that this set of circumstances presented no difficulty whatsoever. When bills from either committee were scheduled to come before the Senate, I paid courtesy calls on the two chairmen. Byrd would receive me personally and it was obvious that he knew what was happening and had resigned himself to his ineffectiveness. In the other case, I was usually received by the chairman's administrative assistant, who was his son. The visits were brief even though we maintained the fiction that this was a form of contact between the central leadership and the committee. I would leave the chairman's office as soon as I could do so decently and head for the Senators in control. From there on in, it was plain sailing. Once protocol had been satisfied, business could be conducted in the mother tongue.

There was one committee, incidentally, where all the

business had to be conducted directly between the chairman—Pat McCarran of Nevada—and Johnson. It was the Senate Judiciary Committee, which had become an independent empire under McCarran's direction. It was a crucial committee because it considered all judicial appointments. Furthermore, McCarran had managed to latch on to the anti-communist cause when the fear of communism was at its height and he had established a reputation for himself as a fierce prosecutor. His colleagues always stepped around him gingerly because he had a temper and was implacable.

During the first two years of the Johnson leadership, the Republicans still exercised nominal Senate control. This meant that the anti-communist forces had shifted their attention from the Judiciary Committee to a Government Operations Subcommittee headed by Joseph R. McCarthy of Wisconsin. This was a man who had no equal as a disruptive force. As a person, he has become fairly well forgotten. But his name lingers on as a synonym for wild, unsubstantiated charges and demagoguery of the most extreme type. For those of us who knew him well, he was a highly implausible con man whose loutish manners were offset by a virile, almost ultramasculine charm. His lack of sincerity about anything he did was apparent to the point of blatancy. Nevertheless, he succeeded in undermining the confidence of millions of Americans in their government and created the suspicion that men of impeccable character, such as General George C. Marshall, were communist dupes.

In retrospect, one of the most interesting characteristics of the McCarthy era was the extreme unlikelihood of his so-called targets. They did not fit the pattern of communists in the United States. His prime victims were generally men and women with Waspish names and a high degree of education. For example, as the number one Soviet agent in the United States he identified Owen Lattimore, a professor at Johns Hopkins University. It is not, of course, possible to prove innocence of a general charge, as Professor Lattimore soon discovered. But the charges against him were ridiculous to the point of absurdity.

The man who really made McCarthy's audiences roar, however, was Dean Acheson, Secretary of State under Harry S Truman. Acheson was probably the most hardline of the anti-communists in the entire American foreign policy establishment. He was also the quintessential WASP, a product of the Eastern Ivy League schools, who had a finely honed mind and absolutely no patience whatsoever with fools. In appearance, he resembled the classic *Chicago Tribune* caricature of a cookie-pushing, striped pants diplomat with an expression on his face that seemed to indicate a foul odor assailing his nostrils. To McCarthy, he became the "Red Dean" and his policies were described as "Dean Acheson's Cowardly School of Communist Containment." Unfortunately for Acheson, at the time Alger Hiss was convicted for lying about communist espionage, he had said: "I will not turn my back on Alger Hiss." It was obvious from the context of the remark that he meant he would not kick a man when he was down and had he said it that way, he would have been a national hero. To McCarthy and his followers, however, it meant that he condoned the activities of Soviet spies.

There was no evidence that any reasonable person could take seriously that involved Acheson with communist activities. There was a good deal of evidence that he was an implacable adversary to the Soviet Union and that all his policies were devoted to efforts to contain Russian expansion. However, there was also a solid mass of evidence that there was a high level of Soviet espionage activity in the United States—so high that it had penetrated the supposedly secure project for making the atomic bomb. Much of the evidence also implicated intellectuals who in the 1930s had become embroiled in communist activities—not because they were Marxists but because the Communist Party had been one of the first organizations to take a firm anti-Fascist stand. In my college days, many students who had absolutely no bent toward Marxism joined the Young Communist League to express their support of the People's Front government in Spain against General Franco and his Fascist and Nazi backers.

McCarthy had nothing whatsoever to do with any of the investigations that had put the spotlight on genuine communists. But he was a public relations genius. One of his techniques was to couple the names of his targets with names that had been turned up in more carefully conducted inquiries. This gave an air of verisimilitude to what he was saying and, eventually, most of his followers came to believe that he was the moving spirit in all the exposés. Once he had established this point, it was all clear sailing. After that, he did not *need* evidence. All he needed were characters who fit the prejudices of his audience, and Acheson fit that role perfectly.

Eisenhower's election had put something of a damper on the McCarthy communist spy hunt. It was one thing to make charges of government infiltration under Democratic Presidents. It was another thing altogether to make those charges under a Republican President—especially one of such tremendous popularity. The McCarthy investigation went into a low key. He was forced to content himself with elaborate hearings on such cases as a communist who, as a dentist, had been promoted from captain to major. The episode involved nothing but an administrative army foul-up of a variety familiar to anyone who has ever spent time in a company orderly room. But McCarthy managed to make it look as though he had uncovered a major Soviet conspiracy to infiltrate the military. High-ranking officers, some with distinguished military records, were called before his committee and raked mercilessly over the coals. Although he did not realize it himself, his act was beginning to wear thin. He was building too much on sheer trivialities and it did not set well. He was making the mistake of forcing conservatives to take sides against him. The climax came when he bullied a black woman who served food in a government cafeteria. Senator McClellan of Arkansas, one of the most conservative members of the Senate, objected publicly to the rather preposterous charges made against her on the basis of anonymous informants. It was obvious that the McCarthy strength was ebbing.

Nevertheless, he was still a potent force that had to be dealt with somehow. There were some factors that dictated the only possible strategy that would work. It was to make clear that the McCarthy charges had very little to do with communism and that he himself had no real knowledge of the history of the Marxist movement. This was not quite as simple as it sounds. The McCarthy chapter of the American saga is proof of the well-known truism that when people *want* to believe something they will believe it *regardless of the evidence.* The facts did not matter.

Senator Millard Tydings of Maryland, who lost his Senate seat after conducting an investigation of the original McCarthy charges, proved the point perfectly. Many of the pre-McCarthy communist investigations had accused people of red sympathies because of their *associations* with radicals. The phrase "guilt by association" had become one of the heated points of argumentation between liberals and conservatives. Tydings said that it was totally irrelevant to the McCarthy technique, which he described as "guilt by accusation." It was an apt characterization. However, it did not solve the problem of why so many Americans were willing to believe such flimsy charges.

Very important clues were provided by the streams of McCarthy supporters who crowded into the Capitol almost every day. To argue with them was a total waste of time. They were not in Washington for evidence but for target identification. They were in Washington for another reason, also. They were present for vengeance. It was impossible to talk to them for any length of time without turning up a deep sense of grievance. They were of many different backgrounds—Irish-Americans; Italian-Americans; German-Americans; small-town Americans; steel- and textile-mill worker Americans. Their speech ranged over a wide spectrum of accents from broken English and Brooklynese to Southern drawls. But they had one thing in common. They all felt that they had been snooted by Ivy League intellectuals and they were delighted to learn that these people were questionable Americans. In my judgment, this was the key to the McCarthy phenomenon. He was pillorying the WASP.

It is difficult so many years after the post–World War II era to realize the intensity of ethnic discrimination in the twenties and the thirties. When I was a child, an Italian was a wop; an Irishman was a mick; a German was a squarehead or a kraut; Hispanics were greasers; Poles were Polacks; and dumb Swede was treated as one word. Blackface comedians performed on the vaudeville stages depicting blacks whose only positive desires were to avoid work and eat watermelon. Their Jewish counterparts spent all their time trying to eat ham (pronounced "hem"), when the rabbi wasn't looking, and to fleece the Gentile at every opportunity. A leading newspaper cartoon of the day—"Maggie and Jiggs"—portrayed the life of an Irish family that had become wealthy. The "humor" involved Maggie's pathetic attempts to attain a social position equal to her husband's economic position and Jiggs's common-sense attitude toward life, which involved the Pipe Fitter's Ball and a plate of corned beef and cabbage at Dinty Moore's. Obviously, he "knew his place" even if Maggie did not.

What may have been the most significant form of discrimination was presented in the apartment house ads. All of them specified "white only" (blacks were supposed to know where to go); many of them specified "white, Gentile only"; and a substantial number specified "white, Anglo-Saxon, Protestant only." The message was clear. The only segment of society that was completely free from the cruelties of ethnic discrimination was the WASP. In the small towns and the rural areas, however, even they felt the lash. To work in a North Carolina textile mill was to be a "linthead" and to plow forty acres or so with a mule was to be a "redneck." The lintheads and the rednecks contrasted sharply with the "quality folks" who had inherited the huge plantations from those who had gotten here first. In short, ours was a society with an aristocracy and it was creating resentments that bore a strong resemblance to those of the Jacquerie of France.

Flashes of this resentment emerged in the twenties and the thirties. One example was the successful mayoralty campaign of William Hale ("Big Bill the Builder") Thompson in 1924. His major campaign plank was a promise to take the first boat to England, if elected, and "punch King George in the snoot." To most of the commentators it was a clownish act and the fact that it worked was evidence that the voters had lost their senses. They did not look beneath the surface. Had they done so, they would have discovered that Big Bill knew what he was doing—and so did the voters. They did not really expect him to take a boat to England and punch the king. But it was such a wonderful feeling to watch the Sassenach squirm.

There was another example in North Carolina in the thirties when Robert Rice Reynolds—appropriately a native of Buncombe County—ran for the Senate on a platform charging that his opponent ate "fish eggs from Red Soviet Russia." This, of course, was only a part of an act in which the major accusation was that his opponent— Cameron Morrison, of aristocratic stock—had turned his back on his state and adopted the effete mannerisms of Northeastern high society. Again, even though it sounds ridiculous, Reynolds knew what he was doing and so did the voters. They were "getting their own back" and it was worth it to them for the man in the "house on the hill" (the phrase used throughout the South to describe the plantation mansions) to get his comeuppance.

World War II had a dampening effect on ethnic—

though not racial—discrimination. Too many Americans learned to rely on too many other Americans for the kind of cooperation that makes the difference between life and death. The cause of survival displaced the cause of ethnic antagonism.

The cause of the resentments remained, however, and McCarthy had learned how to tap them for his own purposes. Whether this was a conscious or an unconscious strategy on his part, I do not know. I suspect he was just playing it by instinct. But his instincts were valid. He himself obviously resented the elitists of America and he knew how to weed out others of a similar mind and lead them in demonstrations against established society. Where he would have led them ultimately is a matter of speculation. Joseph McCarthy was not a serious politician with goals and programs. He regarded the political world as an arena in which men and women competed against each other, and even though McCarthy and I lived in the same apartment building and saw each other frequently, I never detected in him any real desire to "do something" about society. This is why he left no organization or movement behind him.

The problem was a subtle one. With the exception of Millard Tydings, no one in the Senate had argued with him except the liberals. Conservatives generally had stayed out of it—Republicans because they thought he was setting up the Democratic Party for defeat and Southern and Western Democrats because they reserved all their arguments for legislation. The liberals had confined themselves to logic, a totally ineffective tactic. They had failed to realize that logic was irrelevant because it could only demonstrate that McCarthy had not proven any of his charges. Proving charges was not the McCarthy goal. The real objective was to make aristocratic WASPs squirm and as long as he could do that, his followers were proof against evidence. Furthermore, as long as the attacks came *only* from liberals, they actually strengthened McCarthy. Most of the McCarthyites had suspected for years that there was an alliance between liberalism and communism. In their eyes, the liberal response proved the point.

It was apparent that there was only one strategy that could be effective. It was to convert the controversy from one of McCarthy versus the liberals to McCarthy versus the Senate. That could not be done as long as conservatives remained aloof. The problem of bringing them in was solved by McCarthy himself. He had mistaken the silence of the Southern and Western conservatives for fear. It was the biggest mistake of his life. He gratuitously attacked Senator Carl Hayden of Arizona, the Dean of the Senate, who had been a member of the Congress (first in the House of Representatives) since Arizona became a state in 1913. Virtually every Democratic Senator was beholden to Hayden for something. He was chairman of the Senate Appropriatons Committee, ranking member of the Senate Rules Committee and chairman of the Senate Democratic Steering Committee, which assigned committee seats for members of his party. He was responsible for the dispensing of patronage and for office and furniture assignments. All of these responsibilities had been handled so deftly that he had no enemies. To attack him, in the eyes of his colleagues, was to attack the Senate itself.

In another book (*Lyndon B. Johnson, A Memoir*), I have set forth in detail the strategy that resulted in the censure of

McCarthy. Basically, it consisted of pitting him against the whole Senate. The committee that handled the censure resolution consisted of two Southern and one Western Democrat and three Western Republicans. No one noticed that one of the Democrats (Senator Sam Ervin of North Carolina) was a graduate of the Harvard Law School. He was too much of a "country boy" to be mistaken for an "effete Eastern snob." Many of McCarthy's followers were not convinced by the censure resolution that there was anything wrong with their hero. But it took the heart out of him and out of his campaign. Had he pursued some real goals, no matter how unworthy, he might have survived because he was a man of tremendous talent. But when a man's only objective in life is to beat other people, any defeat is disastrous.

Joe's end was messy and maudlin. For most of his life, he had been a light drinker. After the censure, he began to hit the bottle heavily and it was apparent in his appearance. About a year after the censure, I saw him for the last time. I had worked late in the evening and had driven my secretary to her apartment in an area of Capitol Hill where the streets were deserted. There had been a few muggings at the time and I got out of my automobile to be certain that she could enter her building safely. As I stood on the curb, a mud-plastered car pulled up in front of me and out rolled something round and black and squishy, reeking of alcohol. "How d'ya like my new car, George," the apparition said. "I just drove it in from Detroit." It was Joe McCarthy. He died a few months later.

The actual censure was handled outside of the regular session of the Senate in 1954. By that time, Johnson's leadership of the Senate had been firmly established. He had unified the Democrats and divided the Republicans. Even before the election, all of the odds pointed to a Democratic victory—albeit one that would be slim—in both houses. The elements of unified leadership had been put in place and the censure of Joe McCarthy had removed the most disruptive element. The stage was set for the spectacular production that was to follow.

10

Preliminary
Maneuvering

The demise of the Republican–Southern Democratic coalition, the final period placed on the McCarthy saga, and the tacit agreement with Eisenhower all cleared the way for the Democratic leadership. There was one other factor, however, of equal—perhaps greater—importance. It was the existence of a large number of issues that had ripened to a point where they were ready for some variety of settlement. Their time had come.

When Lyndon B. Johnson assumed the leadership in 1953, there had been little or no action on domestic legislation since the mid-thirties. Roosevelt's "court packing" bill and the "purge campaign" that followed it in 1938 had disrupted normal relationships in the Senate and the House of Representatives. The early forties were taken up with war and the late forties with conversion back to

146

peace and with the beginnings of the "cold war." The late forties bogged us down in Korea and opened up the McCarthy era. All of these situations placed a damper on legislative activity. But they did not slow down the rate at which problems were accumulating. Increasing population pressures had provided needs for education, housing, health research, and social services on a scale heretofore unknown. In addition, civil rights had become too insistent to be longer ignored.

Senator Russell once remarked to me that Congress should only meet to legislate on basic domestic problems every ten years and that it should "pass everything in sight" at such meetings. In between, he thought, it should come together each year only to handle the appropriations. His fundamental concept was that a stream of social legislation year after year was bound to be upsetting to the Executive agencies who are charged with carrying out the laws. In his judgment, they needed time to learn how to make the laws work. Furthermore, laws should not be passed before the public has really had a chance to become familiar with the issues.

By 1952, the public had been allowed plenty of time to become familiar with the issues. There was a recognition that things had to be done, accompanied by a desire to have them done sensibly. The pace of the Truman era had been frenetic. The Eisenhower presence was calming. Astute leadership could take advantage of the situation to pass almost anything for which a case could be made—provided that he did not object. Everything began to fall into place.

One of the important factors in the strategy of the Democratic leadership was the character of the Republican leaders during the crucial years. When Congress met in 1953 after the Eisenhower victory, Taft assumed the Senate leadership himself. This was one of the factors that made the Johnson strategy so attractive. The label "isolationist" did not wholly fit Taft even though he had generally been associated with the isolationist bloc in the maneuverings that preceded World War II. However, he had encouraged McCarthy in the latter's search for communists in the State Department and he was quite willing to use the Senate as a sounding board for condemning the activities of past Democratic administrations in world affairs. It did not make too much difference to him that President Eisenhower had played such a key role in those activities as to be indistinguishable from the Democratic foreign establishment.

Had Taft and Eisenhower ever come to a real meeting of the minds, the combination would have been formidable. No one could doubt Taft's ability nor discount his position as the "Mr. Republican" of the Senate. He was skilled in the arts of legislation and had he been around in later years, Lyndon Johnson would not have been able to pass so many Democratic measures on the domestic front. His only real impact during the Eisenhower administration was to precipitate the foreign policy clashes that the Democrats seized upon to build the picture of the need to defend the President from members of his own party. Taft died in 1953 when the spotlight was on international relations. He was replaced by Senator William Knowland of California, an altogether different type of man.

It would be difficult to conceive of any Republican more perfectly adapted to the Johnson strategy than Bill Knowland. He was a bundle of contradictions. The man had a high level of intelligence and he was ruggedly honest. But he was also a shy, straight-line thinker who was no match for the wiles of men like Johnson, Russell, or Kerr. What was most important was his concept of the leadership. He regarded the post as a position from which righteous banners were to be raised rather than a command center for welding the Republicans into a cohesive fighting force. He was not a member of the radical right but he was mildly conservative. What is more important is that he was one of the strongest supporters in the Senate of Chiang Kai-shek and the Chinese Nationalist regime. This inevitably placed him in conflict with the White House, where the feeling that Chiang was a loser was ill-concealed.

Knowland regarded as somehow unworthy the kind of maneuvering that was essential to holding parliamentary factions together. He had a "right must prevail" approach to politics and thought that the proper practice of the art was to educate his colleagues on the truth of his philosophies. I found rather appealing his practice of leaving the Republican leader's desk in the front of the chamber and retiring to one in the rear whenever he was set to make a speech opposing Eisenhower. Somewhere, he had picked up the notion that the Senate leader was the President's leader and should step aside every time he was unable to carry the President's banner.

The net result was to pave the way for the second stage of the Democratic strategy: to take Presidential proposals and put a Democratic stamp upon them. Had Taft remained in the Senate, this would have been a difficult feat. It was made possible because the Republican leadership under Knowland was raising banners rather than promoting party unity. Of course, it required some fine-tuning. Careful estimates had to be made of how far the Democrats could go without provoking the Eisenhower veto, which was deadly. This was complicated by the attitude of many of the liberal Democrats who preferred the issue to the achievement. They sought to push issues to the veto point on the theory that this would give them ammunition for the next campaign. The Democratic leadership saw the situation in a different manner. In Johnson's eyes, it was the continual pushing of issues without bringing anything to achievement that had toppled the Truman administration. He was convinced that the Democrats needed to demonstrate responsible accomplishment in order to return to power. And if that record could be made with Republicans visibly divided, so much the better.

At this point, a few reflections on the nature of President-Congress relationships are in order. Very few successful bills originate in Congress. When they do, they are usually proposals to change the Constitution—such as the Bricker amendment of 1954—or sweeping measures espousing a philosophy at odds with the occupant of the White House—such as the Subversive Activities Control Act of the early 1950s. The true legislative agenda is set by the President in the proposals he sends to the House and Senate. Some of his requests are defeated totally; some are amended and passed; some are amended so substantially that they run counter to what he asked. But the trigger that sets the debate and the parliamentary process into motion is the Presidential request. During all the years I was close to the Congress, the only important measures I can recall that began on Capitol Hill were the Taft-Hartley Labor Relations Act; the Subversive Activities Control Act; some restrictive immigration acts; the two-term limitation on the Presidency; and the act that established the National Aeronautics and Space Administration. (It should be added that President Eisenhower indicated he would support the latter even before it was passed. The others were passed over Presidential vetoes.)

Three of these measures were possible only because of the Republican–Southern Democratic coalition. This afforded the necessary majority to override an unpopular President. The Democrats in 1953 and 1954—or at any other time in the decade—did not have such majorities. The idea of introducing *Democratic* bills was totally impractical. Such a practice would have had the tendency to unify the Republican side of the aisle and the net effect would have been a series of vetoes with the Democrats appearing solely as men playing politics. It would have been a foolish strategy.

The practice of concentration on the modification of Presidential bills, however, had much to commend it. In the first place, amendment is a normal activity of Congress. It does not look like partisan, political strategy even when it is. In the second place, it *did* pit Democrats against Republicans and thus helped work off some of the belligerency of the activists. Thirdly, it was certain to meet with some degree of success because the President himself was under obligation to the Democrats of Congress. He would veto anything that in his judgment went too far but he could also be counted upon to be elastic in his judgments on how far was too far.

To me, this was one of the most fascinating periods of my years around the Senate. Eisenhower and the Democrats were *not* in cahoots. To my personal knowledge, there was never any meeting between the Democratic leaders and the President that was not attended by the Republicans. The game was played at arm's length—actually at the length of Pennsylvania Avenue from Capitol Hill to the White House. But it worked without either side sacrificing any degree of political independence. The Democrats were helping Eisenhower and Eisenhower was helping the Democrats but both sides were acting in their own self-interest and at no point was the separation of the two parties breached.

There is an ancient Greek account of the trading that went on between the Phoenicians and the people of Cornwall. The Phoenicians badly needed tin, which did not exist in their part of the world. The people of Cornwall badly needed manufactured goods because their level of civilization was not high. They were suspicious of each other—or at least they wished to deal with the minimum of contact possible. The system that was worked out represented barter at its crudest level.

The Phoenicians would come ashore at Cornwall and leave their trade goods on the beach. Then they would withdraw and their ships would move out of sight from land. Once they could no longer be seen, the people of Cornwall would stack what they regarded as an equivalent amount of tin and retreat into the interior. After a day or two, the Phoenicians would come ashore and, if they were satisfied, would load the tin on their galleys and take off, leaving the trade goods behind. If they were not satisfied, they would give the people of Cornwall a chance to supplement their first bid. The process could go on for weeks. But apparently it satisfied both parties. Each side could get what it wanted without what was obviously considered the unpleasant experience of personal contact.

Some such arrangement was necessary if the Democrats were to be effective. Eisenhower demonstrated from the beginning that he could get whatever he really wanted in the field of domestic legislation. Early in his administration, he went to bat for a fundamental change in agricultural legislation—an area in which the Democrats thought they had enough strength to maintain the laws that had been passed under their Presidents. It is worth taking a closer look at the underlying factors that determined the outcome as, again, it illustrates the type of forces that ultimately determine action in the Senate.

The key to the farm programs of Franklin D. Roosevelt and Harry S Truman had been the parity concept. This held that a farmer was entitled to the same purchasing power from the proceeds of selling his crop that he had received during an earlier period when there was a favorable ratio between farm income and farm expenses. A simple way of looking at it is that if a bushel of wheat would buy a pair of overalls in 1912, a bushel of wheat should be able to buy a pair of overalls in 1952.

The concept was applied only to what were termed "the basic commodities"—defined as wheat, corn, cotton, tobacco, and rice. The definitions were probably put together by political demographers, who understood the electoral strength of the producers of those crops, rather than economists because parity had a strength in the Senate that for many years had been unbeatable. Of course, the farmer was not guaranteed full parity—although there were advocates of such a move. What he could get was ninety percent of parity guarantees, provided that he

153

went through a series of moves. Basically, these depended upon elections that were held whenever a bumper crop in any of the "basics" threatened to depress prices. The producers (of course, only the producers affected were included in the vote and they had to operate in certain areas of the nation designated as "commercial") were given a choice between acreage restrictions on their crops or unlimited production. If they voted for acreage restrictions, they could then borrow ninety percent of the parity price from the government on the harvest from their allotted acreage and the production would go into the hands of the federal authorities, who would put it under seal. If the price that year should go sufficiently high to justify the move, the farmers could pay back the loan, take possession of their commodities and sell them on the open market. Should prices remain low, they would merely forfeit their collateral.

The economic validity of the parity support program had been in dispute from the very beginning. There were critics who maintained that it favored the huge factory-type farms and did practically nothing for the small farmers who had provided the rationale for its existence. There were others who said that the cost was staggering and that it represented a subsidy that went far beyond anything made available to other elements of our society. These attacks made no dent whatsoever. The "commercial areas" for the basic crops extended over so many states that a solid phalanx of Senators from all of the nation except the Northeast was ready to repel all boarders. The parity program was a sacred cow. Two of its principal backers had been Representative Frank Pace of Georgia and Representative Clifford Hope of Kansas, and throughout Capitol Hill an only partially humorous jingle ran: "Pace, Hope and Parity conquers all!" The last time anyone had sought to play games with the program was during the Republican-controlled Eightieth Congress, which did not appropriate enough money for storage facilities in 1948. The result was that Truman carried farm states that had voted Republican consistently since the Civil War.

When Eisenhower proposed a flexible support program, it was widely believed that he would lose this battle with Congress. Why he did it was somewhat of a mystery at first. During the campaign, he had pledged himself to maintain the ninety percent concept. It came as something of a shock when he unveiled his proposal to place the loans on a sliding scale up to eighty percent with the amount decreasing as the amount of crop surplus grew. In other words, the more desperate the need, the less would be the loans to the producers.

The key to the situation was Eisenhower's Secretary of Agriculture, Ezra Taft Benson, a devout Mormon who felt that all of his projects in life should be related to a semidivine mission. He had a very close friend in Aled Davies, the representative of the American Meat Institute and one of the shrewdest lobbyists that ever came to Washington. Whether Davies or someone else introduced Benson to the flexible parity concept, no one will ever know. But Davies did realize that basic changes in agriculture had eroded the strength of the fixed price support program and that its assumed invulnerability was little more than a facade. There is no doubt in my mind that the strategy that was planned originated in his mind. Benson was too direct and straightforward a man to understand parliamentary ma-

155

neuvering. His support of his proposal was messianic rather than Machiavellian.

The American Meat Institute had never been too happy with fixed price supports simply because they kept feed grain prices at a fairly high level. This meant a higher price for meat and a threat to the profits of the meat packers. They did not really care about cotton, rice, or tobacco. But they had a direct interest in corn and high prices for wheat meant high prices for oats, barley, sorghums, and others that were known as "small feed grains." However, for many years the AMI did not have the political clout to offset the parity farm bloc. The principal area for cattle production was Texas and other Southern states where cotton was equally important and the hog-producing areas were identical to the commercial corn-producing area.

After World War II, however, subtle shifts began to take place in the economics of farming. The flow had been from the rangelands of the South and the Southwest to feed lots in the North and then to the huge packing centers of Omaha, Chicago, and Kansas City. After the war, cattle producers began to move North and become economically important, which meant, ultimately, politically important also. In addition, the consolidation trend had set in for agriculture and the total percentage of people devoted to farming had begun to diminish. Those areas where the small farm was still economically viable were devoted almost entirely to truck farming—a type to which the parity concept did not apply. In short, the political base for the parity farm bloc was not only shrinking but what was left was being diluted by producers who had no interest in parity.

In Washington, Aled Davies assiduously cultivated his senatorial friends, spreading the gospel that "the future of agriculture lies in the meat animal." (This is a direct quote because he tried it on me for size.) It was a period in which meat production was very profitable, whereas the basic crops—except for tobacco and rice—were all in trouble. The war had put an end to the lush export market for cotton. Wheat production had surged upward in other nations competing for the world market. There had been shifts in the national taste away from pork and toward beef and this had impinged upon feed corn. The prospect of establishing a profitable beef production industry in the Northern states was very attractive to many legislators. Senators from states where parity had no impact had never been very happy with the program, as they blamed it for higher prices in their urban food markets.

Without the prestige of Dwight D. Eisenhower, the fixed price supports would probably have lasted a few more years. But that would merely have meant delay. The conditions that had built the unbeatable farm bloc had disappeared and it broke up as soon as a reputable figure raised a banner against it. The most fascinating aspect of the whole controversy to me, however, was the illustration of the length of time it takes people to see reality. The legend of parity persisted long after the strength had evaporated, and very practical politicians failed to recognize the truth until it was too late.

The victory on the farm bill dampened the enthusiasm of those who wanted to challenge Eisenhower directly. His victory was all the more remarkable in that it flew in the face of the position he himself had taken during the campaign and nobody held it against him. The Democrats tried to make the point that he had gone back on his word, only to discover that nobody cared. The American people liked Ike and did not care what he said or whether he contradicted himself.

The farm bill made more than clear the validity of the Democratic leadership strategy. Nothing was to be gained by direct confrontation, although sometimes it could not be avoided. However, it was possible to take most Eisenhower proposals and modify them into bills that were substantially Democratic. Most important of all, the remnants of the isolationist movement were still so strong in the Republican Party that it was easily possible to set Republican legislators against him on foreign policy issues and to make it clear to the public that he was being rescued by the Democrats. Finally, the belligerent instincts of those who wanted to fight Ike could be satisfied by turning them loose on White House appointments. During his eight years in office, Eisenhower placed into high federal positions far too many businessmen who did not understand the world of government in which practices that are quite common in industry can look quite nefarious.

Of course, this was not a strategy that could defeat Eisenhower running for reelection in 1956. On that, however, there was a deliberate judgment holding that he was unlikely to be beaten under any circumstances. On that premise, the obvious course was to spend the time implanting in the public consciousness the idea that Republicans were irresponsible and that the GOP label on Ike had nothing to do with reality. It was a strategy that worked.

11

Back in the Majority

The 1954 elections produced Democratic majorities for both the House and the Senate. Lyndon Johnson and his supporters pointed to the outcome as evidence of the validity of the leadership strategy. The forthcoming Congress, however, did not run smoothly. There were simply too many would-be Presidential candidates on the Democratic side of the aisle. Their primary goal was not to make the Republican Party look bad but to make President Eisenhower look bad. They had come to the conclusion that 1956 was *their* year for the Presidential nomination and, obviously, it was not going to be worth much unless Eisenhower could be toppled from his pedestal.

In retrospect, it is rather interesting that the two Democrats in the Senate who were to achieve the Presidency—

Kennedy and Johnson—did not figure in the speculation of that period. The active candidates were Estes M. Kefauver of Tennessee; Robert Kerr of Oklahoma; and Stuart Symington of Missouri. Of the three, Kefauver shone the most brightly and had the least influence in the Senate.

The other two men were of quite a different type. Both were wealthy but Kerr had made his pile by striking it rich in oil wildcatting, whereas Symington had been a manufacturer. The difference in their economic backgrounds was reflected in their temperaments. Politically, Kerr was something of a pirate—a man who could demolish a political opponent with a single cutting speech. He had an unerring instinct for the jugular and could turn defeat into victory at the most unexpected time and place. It is worth recounting one episode to illustrate the kind of man involved. It took place in 1950 when his Oklahoma colleague A. S. "Mike" Monroney entered the race for his reelection.

Monroney found himself pitted against a Baptist preacher, the Reverend William H. Alexander. Alexander was a widely known evangelist who told his congregation on Sunday that he had "wrestled with the Lord" in his study on the preceding night and been ordered to get the Democratic nomination for the Senate. Apparently he had misunderstood some of the Lord's instructions because he finished by securing the Republican nomination. When it came to questions of digging up votes, however, his understanding was very keen. He mounted an attack upon Monroney based upon the assumption that the Lord wanted Alexander in the Senate and, just in case that was not a sufficient endorsement, he brought the singing cow-boy star Roy Rogers and his horse, Trigger, into Oklahoma to campaign for him. It was a good show and voters responded enthusiastically. It was widely believed that Monroney was headed for defeat.

Kerr had no desire to share the Oklahoma senatorial limelight with the Reverend Mr. Alexander. He much preferred Mike Monroney, an earnest, quiet man with little or no sense of public relations. He was obviously bewildered by his opponent and did not have the faintest idea of how to handle the situation. Kerr obliged at the Democratic state convention. His opening remarks, in a speech that became a classic in the political lore of the Southwest, began by recalling the statement that the Lord had wrestled with Alexander and ordered him to get the Democratic nomination. Now, he pointed out, Alexander was running on the Republican ticket, which raised the question of "who entered the Rev. Alexander's study late at night and wrestled with him and ordered him to disobey the clear commands of the Lord." The crowd whooped and hollered as Kerr developed his theme. Did the creature who wrestled with Alexander have forked hooves and a tail? Did he have horns protruding from his forehead? Was there an odor of brimstone left in the study, which Alexander had to dissipate the next morning? The final thrust involved Roy Rogers and Trigger. Trigger, Kerr said, looked more like a horse than the Rev. Alexander looked like a Senator. "But the people of Oklahoma can't send a horse to the Senate," he concluded. "Not even half a horse."

This was typical Kerr oratory and it could be devastating. It was offset, however, by his failure to understand modern communications techniques. In this field, he was no match for Kefauver. The difference between the two men was illustrated in the Presidential primaries in Nebraska in 1956. The state, at that time, had an unusual primary system in which voters would indicate their preference for a Presidential candidate on one ballot but vote for Democratic delegates to the national convention on another ballot. Both Kerr and Kefauver entered the Nebraska race. Kefauver won the Presidential preference vote overwhelmingly. But Kerr won virtually all the delegates to the national convention. He had made a series of deals that put very popular local people on his slates and they carried the day. It should be added that Nebraska and Oklahoma supplied virtually all his delegates, and his entire convention strategy was to emphasize that he had been born in a genuine log cabin. It was not a very effective appeal. Not enough other Americans had been born in log cabins to establish any feeling of affinity.

Nobody had any anecdotes about Symington. But had anyone just looked at the record, he would unquestionably have been the leading candidate. He had been a distinguished Secretary of the Air Force and a solid businessman who had demonstrated a capacity to administer large enterprises effectively. He had a knack for assembling competent staffs and the people working for him were universally rated among the top aides on Capitol Hill. He was incapable of making the big splash required by modern campaigning and his only achievement was to help keep Missouri out of the Kefauver grasp.

The approaching election of 1956 had another effect, however, which governed much of that which was done by the Democratic leadership. It was the prospect of major defections from the Democratic camp out of the

Southern delegations. Nowhere was the threat greater than in Texas, the home state of the Democratic leader. In 1952, Governor Allan Shivers of Texas had succeeded in taking the Texas Democratic delegation and using it to build support for Eisenhower on the basis of the so-called tidelands issue. The emotions on that argument were still running high and it was obvious that Shivers was planning to use the same strategy in 1956.

At the present time, it seems fantastic that such an issue could stir such deep emotions. It involved the question of whether the seaward boundaries of Texas extended for three miles or three marine leagues (about ten and one-half miles) beyond the low tide mark into the Gulf of Mexico. The legal issues were abstruse and about as difficult to determine as the question of how many angels can dance on the head of a pin. It was agreed that every other state (or at least almost every other state) had such jurisdiction for three miles only and that the federal government had full sovereignty from there on out to the continental shelf. Texas, however, had entered the union under a treaty that allowed it to keep its own public lands. While still a nation, Texas had set the three marine leagues boundary mark and claimed that this had not been vitiated by its merger with the United States.

For a long period of time, nobody really cared except for a small coterie of puzzle addicts who today would be involved in high-IQ trivia quiz games. But rich oil strikes in the Gulf of Mexico made a difference. The so-called tidelands began to look like a valuable prize and sides were drawn up quickly. In Texas, the construction of public schools was financed by revenues from oil lands and this led residents of the state to believe that a battle for the tidelands was a battle for the education of their children. For the rest of the nation, the Texas oilmen—whether fairly or unfairly—had become a national stereotype symbolizing arrogance, greed, and vulgarity, and it was assumed that the battle for the tidelands was a steal. Probably never before in history has so much emotion been aroused over about six and a half miles of salt water that to this day has produced no oil.

For Johnson, the tidelands issue was excruciating torture. Both he and his counterpart in the House of Representatives—Speaker Sam Rayburn—had gotten their fingers burned in negotiating a compromise during the early days of the controversy. It was a sensible move that would have accepted the jurisdiction of the federal government over the underwater lands beyond the three-mile limit but would have granted Texas one-third of the revenues from any oil in that area. The answer from Texas was a resounding "No!" The Texans wanted their land and were not at all interested in a deal that would merely get their state some money. In vain, Johnson and Rayburn pleaded that one-third of something was better than three-thirds of nothing but the mathematics did not appeal.

Obviously, the two men had no choice other than to go along with the pro-Texas tidelands stance. Any other posture would have been suicidal. This was well understood by their colleagues in both the House and the Senate and it did not hurt their standing even though it was anathema to the Democratic liberals. But the use of the issue to convert the Texas Democratic Party into a vehicle for Dwight D. Eisenhower was something else again. It meant that Johnson had to pay much closer attention to his

Texas base than he had at any other time in the past. For once, the internal Democratic Party problems of the Lone Star State were very much on his mind. What he did, as a result, was to focus as much attention as he could on purely Texas or Southwest regional issues without losing the strength he had gained among his Northern colleagues by his astute leadership on such questions as housing, health, and education. This led to a very heavy concentration on the natural gas bill.

As is true of most economic issues, the natural gas bill involved complex subtleties that were presented to the public in a simplified form. The real issues seldom surfaced—to a great degree because of the ineptitude of Texas oilmen and the skill of Northern utility companies in public relations. The real battle was between those two groups over whether gas should be regulated at the wellhead or the delivery point, but outside of the gas-producing states it appeared to be (and to some extent was) a clash between producers and consumers over a monopoly product. In Texas, the emotional appeal stemmed from the close ties between gas and oil production (for a long time, gas was merely a waste product from oil wells). In the North, the emotional appeal was related directly to the severity of the winters and the vital necessity of finding heating sources in areas that produced very little fuel other than timber. The intensity of feeling made it impossible to hold a rational discussion of the logical arguments that could be marshaled on both sides.

The necessity of shoring up the Texas party base against mass defection in 1956 led Lyndon B. Johnson to risk his standing in the North by embracing Texas issues even when they were unpopular with most elements of the national Democratic Party. He had to have a victory under his belt for the home folks but it had to be one that would not destroy the bridges he had built in other directions. It was obvious that there could be no victory on the tidelands question. So the Natural Gas Act was the only alternative. Despite the opposition to it from Democratic Party liberals, there were enough votes in the Senate to pass the measure. The real question was the extent to which his active plugging of the legislation would jeopardize his national standing.

There were a number of circumstances that made the selection of the gas act preferable to another bout over tidelands. For one thing, the House of Representatives passed a Texas-style bill in 1955 and the Senate Commerce Committee sent a similar—but separate—measure to the Senate floor the same year. It was not considered, however, in view of the somewhat shortened session that resulted from Lyndon Johnson's heart attack in July. Nevertheless, it was on the calendar and ready for consideration. The votes were available for passage and it would have been a safe assurance of Texas party loyalty during the forthcoming Presidential campaign.

There has been considerable speculation as to whether Johnson's heart attack was precipitated by contemplation of the problems involved in that bill. Personally, I doubt it. However, the heart attack did set the stage for him to kick off the legislative struggle under circumstances best calculated to minimize the political damage that it did to him.

The doctors who attended Johnson ruled that he could make one major speech during the fall season after he went back to the ranch to recuperate. For a number of reasons, this speech had to be delivered at Lake Whitney, a small Texas town with very little access other than country roads. Johnson went into high gear and set machinery in motion that led people to fly into Whitney from all over Texas. The speech was one of his best performances—an emotional appeal for Democratic loyalty that virtually hypnotized his audience. Few of them noticed that part of the speech that captured national headlines the next day. It was the presentation of a Democratic legislative program that included among its thirteen points a natural gas bill.

It was a masterly bit of strategy. His thirteen points included something for everybody—organized labor, farmers, liberals, and progressives. Most of it was in the Populist tradition. It could not be repudiated as a whole by his Northern colleagues nor did they want to carp too much over the natural gas bill out of fear of distracting attention from the other parts of the program. Finally, they did not want to be put in the position of arguing too strongly with a man who had been brought so close to death by a massive heart attack.

Unfortunately, the passage of the bill did not go as smoothly. Oil company lobbyists swarmed like crickets through the halls of the Senate and one of them made what Senator Francis Case of South Dakota charged was an outrageous attempt to pay him for his vote. It consisted of a $2,000 campaign contribution that Case described as mammoth by the standards of campaigning in his state. The episode touched off a far-reaching investigation. Nobody went to jail, as the contribution offered to Case was within the terms of the federal campaign financing laws, however questionable may have been the ethics of the proffer. The bill was passed anyway but by that time it had fallen into widespread disrepute. President Eisenhower vetoed the measure with no resulting kickback.

For Lyndon B. Johnson, it would have been impossible to improve upon the outcome, considering the point at which things had started. He had gone to bat for the bill, money marbles and chalk, and Texans could not fault his performance. None of his close friends had been involved in any bribery efforts even though they had been guilty of the garish display of the Texas oil lobbyists, which made them look as though they were guilty of subornation. Finally, the veto had sent the bill down the drain and it was not a law on the books to be used to keep anti-LBJ animosities alive. In the parliamentary world, nothing is buried more deeply in the collective consciousness than a bill that has been defeated and obviously cannot be revived.

The problem still remained, however, of the home base. Allan Shivers had announced early in 1956 that he would not run for reelection as governor. Nevertheless, he still had control of the state machinery and was quite capable—unless he was checked—of swinging the official Democratic Party of Texas to Dwight D. Eisenhower. This would have been disastrous to Johnson's status as a national Democratic leader. He could survive an Eisenhower electoral victory in his home state. But however unfair such an attitude would have been, he would have been blamed by his Northern colleagues if Texas Democrats had placed their organizations behind a Republican.

Actually, in the normal course of events, there was very little he could do about it. Texas, at that time, had a long tradition of separating its politicians between those interested in state office and those who sought seats in the House and the Senate. Generally speaking, there was an unwritten truce between the two groups that they would leave each other alone. There were a few exceptions in which a politician on one track would cross the line and run for another office—such as Price Daniel who managed to get himself elected, in order, Attorney General, Senator, and Governor. But the exceptions were few. An unfortunate corollary of that understanding was that the machinery that selected the delegates to the Democratic National Convention was in control of the men and women on the state political track. Johnson's admitted clout in the United States Senate gave him no leverage whatsoever in state politics. In that respect, he was an outsider.

The same problem was faced by another Texan with a national reputation—Sam Rayburn, Speaker of the House of Representatives. His position as Speaker was somewhat more secure than Johnson's position as floor leader, as Rayburn could truly be described as "beloved" by his House colleagues. In all the years I spent around the Congress, I knew of no one in either branch who commanded so thoroughly the affections of the members. It was close to adoration. Again, however, this was accompanied by a total lack of influence in the state politics of Texas. His position was even weaker than that of LBJ, as he represented a small, sparsely populated rural area that contained no important businessmen looking to him for bills that would solve some of their problems. Johnson at least had the backing of some powerful economic forces in the state.

The solution to the problem came from Rayburn—a

man who did not have Johnson's subtlety in action but who outstripped his junior colleague in conceptual thinking. It was to run Johnson as a "favorite son" candidate in order to get hold of the state's political machinery. It was a daring concept, which had occurred to no one else simply because few people realized that the system that led to the selection of the Texas delegation was vulnerable to a daring raid at the base. The success of the Eisenhower campaign in 1952 had not been fully appreciated by the Democrats because they ascribed the seizure of the Texas Republican Party from its traditional leadership as a matter of ineptitude. They knew that Allan Shivers was not an inept man and, therefore, reasoned that he would gain automatic control.

Johnson was extremely reluctant to enter the battle against Shivers—partly out of the traditional dislike of Congressional types for interfering in Texas state machinery and partly because he overestimated the Shivers strength. Rayburn took care of the question by raising the possibility in such a way that Johnson either had to accept the challenge or look gutless. He accepted the challenge and precipitated the roughest political campaign in which I ever participated. When it was over, the *Time* magazine story on it opened: "Even for Texas, the battle was savage." The outcome, however, was never really in doubt. Shivers had relied too much on the traditional controls of a Texas governor and had not sensed the dawn of a new political era.

His first discovery was that he did not have even the traditional controls. His position had been fatally weakened by his decision not to run for reelection—giving John Connally, who managed the LBJ campaign, an opportunity to call powerful leaders and ask: "Do you want a dead governor or a live Senator?" The message was clearly understood. However, there had been an even more important development. The Eisenhower victory of 1952 had led many Texas Democrats to reassess their position and to conduct some deep studies of the state machinery to determine how to seize control of it. A working alliance was formed known as the Labor-Liberal coalition, which set up an elaborate system of block and precinct captains who patrolled their areas constantly urging their constituents to go to the precinct conventions and vote. For the first time in many years, the precinct conventions all over the state were swamped and Shivers lost them four to one. He carried nothing except a few oil counties (it always came as something of a shock to Northern liberals to discover that Johnson was distrusted by most oilmen) and a few "black belt" counties where blacks outnumbered the whites but did not vote, and whites, who did vote, thought Johnson was too liberal on race questions.

The Johnson "favorite son" candidacy had no appreciable effect upon the outcome of the 1956 Democratic convention. The nomination went predictably to Adlai Stevenson—not because he was the candidate most likely to defeat Eisenhower but because he was the man best calculated to make the party look good in defeat. He could be relied upon for lofty speeches of such great purity that they would not be divisive even when he was taking courageous stands on emotional issues. It felt good to campaign for Stevenson, even though one knew he was not going to win.

There is another aspect of the 1956 convention, however, that is worth a passing thought. It did not alter the shape of Presidential politics in 1956 but it was the launching pad for achievement of the Presidency by two Democrats who had not been considered substantial candidates up to that point—John F. Kennedy and Lyndon B. Johnson. For both of those men, the convention was crucial. And because it played such an important role in their careers, it had a deep effect on the conduct of Congress for the next four years.

For Johnson, the importance of the convention was simply that he had defeated Shivers. In Northern minds, Shivers had become established as a "demagogue"—an entity that was not very well understood but was deeply feared North of the Mason-Dixon line. To defeat a demagogue in any type of an electoral battle was to establish impeccable credentials with the North. It is unlikely that LBJ could have gained acceptance for the White House had it not been for his success in blocking the probability of a second Texas Democratic delegation going over to the Republican camp.

The unexpected boost in the Kennedy fortunes came after the nomination of Stevenson who threw the convention into an uproar by announcing that he was throwing the Vice Presidential nomination open to the delegates. The result was near chaos. Obviously, Kefauver had the most strength among the delegates but no Southern delegation could afford to back him. Again, Johnson found himself faced with a dilemma. It was solved when Senator Albert Gore, the other Tennessee Democrat, announced his candidacy.

For Johnson and the Texas delegation, the Gore candidacy was manna from heaven. He was a moderate conservative who had made no enemies North or South and Johnson endorsed him before he had even finished making a plea for support. However, not having made enemies was an insufficient recommendation for the delegates. Gore was eliminated early, reopening the virtual certainty that Kefauaver would get the nod. At that point, Johnson was able to swing the Texas delegation to John F. Kennedy—a move that would have been impossible at the beginning because of the JFK Catholicism and the anti-"Papist" feeling that still prevailed in the Lone Star State. Between a Catholic and Estes Kefauver, however, many Texans found they would rather vote for the Catholic, a development that started many of them thinking. Kefauver finally won the contest but Kennedy had piled up sufficient votes to attract national attention.

The Senate cannot be considered apart from the 1956 convention. The next four years were to be dominated by Presidential politics simply because Eisenhower could not run for a third term under the Republican-sponsored two-term amendment to the Constitution. This meant that the Democratic candidate in 1960 would have a real chance and a real chance is the kind of situation that brings out the heavy political guns. The Presidential prospects for 1956 had made some impact upon the conduct of the Senate from 1952 on. But it had been a desultory impact compared to what was ahead.

Furthermore, after the 1956 convention, the Senate Republicans achieved degrees of unity that had not been possible after 1952. The death of Taft and the later departure of Knowland removed the strong Eisenhower oppositionists from the leadership to be replaced by Senator Everett Dirksen, a wily pragmatist who had all the legislative skills of Lyndon Johnson. Finally, as 1960 approached, Eisenhower himself became more of a partisan. It was a creeping process that did not reach a climax until the last two years. But the shadows were cast early in 1957 and, as we shall see, they governed what followed.

12

The Pride That Goeth Before the Fall

The two years that followed the 1956 election were the golden years as far as Lyndon Johnson's legislative record was concerned. The Democrats emerged from the hustings with an increased majority—one that was large enough to command but not large enough to be unwieldy. It was a classic example of ticket splitting on the part of the voters. They wanted Ike for President; but they also wanted the kind of Congress that LBJ and his colleague Rayburn had presented to them. One cannot help but wonder whether the people who went to the polls that year were deliberately seeking a balance.

Despite their Presidential sweep, the Republicans were in a sad state of disarray. Without the unifying principle of Robert A. Taft, the conservatives had fragmented into warring factions. The Dewey machine, which had controlled Republican conventions since 1944, was getting long in the tooth. Eisenhower himself had sought to build no personal organization because he did not need it. His personality alone was enough. He had needed the Dewey organization to win the nomination in 1952. But once the convention was behind him, he required nothing but a housekeeping staff to handle schedules, transportation, and contacts with the press.

It is worth noting at this point that the Eisenhower independence from organization marked a turning point in American politics. Roosevelt and Truman had both leaned heavily on the city machines of Tammany, Hague, Kelly, Arvey, and Pendergast. They not only delivered conventions; they delivered crucial votes. This had been a pattern clear back to the last quarter of the nineteenth century. The city machines were a keystone of American politics—especially for the Democratic Party. Republican politics was dominated more by statehouse machines and organizations in rural areas. The basic point of all the machines was that ideology was not foremost in their thinking. They existed primarily to seize and perpetuate organizational control as a way of making a living. Since Eisenhower, the unifying principles of American politics have been ideology and personality. The last election in which political boss support was crucial involved John F. Kennedy and the Cook County (Chicago) machine of Richard Daley, the last of the breed.

It may seem like something of a paradox to state that the 1956 election weakened the Senate Republicans and strengthened the Senate Democrats. But that is exactly what happened. The Republicans had lost the unifying quality that had preceded 1956—the anticipation that Eisenhower would head the ticket at the next election. He was precluded from this by the two-term Constitutional amendment passed during the Republican-controlled Eightieth Congress. The Democrats, on the other hand, had seen (or at least thought they had seen) the tactics of their leadership paying off in terms of an increased majority while the Presidential wing of their party had gone down to defeat—honorable but still a defeat. At the same time, they were still too far away from 1960 to feel the political divisiveness that settles into any political party in the United States when a change in the Presidency is in the cards. They wanted more Johnson-brand leadership and they got it.

In the parlance of gamblers, Johnson was "on a roll" and he shoved in all his chips. Housing, medical research, and public power bills, all substantial, passed almost routinely. In 1958, when a recession had set in, he pushed through a series of highway construction, public works, and housing finance bills at a rate that made him—rather than Eisenhower—appear to be the leader of the country. It was a dazzling display of legislative virtuosity and for the first time the press began to regard him as a serious Presidential possibility. As a person, he became as interesting to correspondents as the President. Reams of copy were produced on his control of the Senate, which even extended to hand signals passed to the clerks on roll calls—a downward shove with his open hands when he wanted them to slow down; a spinning motion with a long forefinger when he wanted them to hurry up. (For those unfamiliar with parliamentary procedures, the slowdown would come when he didn't have the votes but thought he could get them fast; the hustle when he had the votes and wanted them recorded before they could get away.)

The success of his leadership affected the Lyndon Johnson life-style visibly. His office was moved to a luxurious suite on the Senate floor level and visitors entering the outer chamber could not avoid a feeling that they were in the anteroom of Louis XIV. During his early years as leader, he put on a humble-pie act that would have done credit to Ella Cinders. This faded almost overnight and a major task of his staff was to keep the hubris from showing—too much. At one point, speaking on the Senate floor, he referred to the committee chairmen as his "cabinet"—a statement that prompted a large number of newspaper stories speculating upon whether he thought he was already in the White House under a system in which elections had become superfluous. After one spectacular triumph, a reporter with a taste for Shakespeare said to me: "This Johnson doth bestride the narrow world like a Colossus. . . ." The language was florid but it was not at all difficult to agree with the sentiment.

Most of the measures that were passed reflected essentially the Populist side of the New Deal. But there were two that departed from the past and from the normal patterns of legislative behavior. They were the Civil Rights Act of 1957 and the National Aeronautics and Space Act of 1958. Both were fascinating in that they reflected what could be done when political currents favored strong Congressional leadership. Both were historic in the sense that they changed patterns of life in the United States and shaped the future in a major way.

The Civil Rights Act has been analyzed in detail in other works and the analysis need not be repeated here. Basically, it was a question of splitting the far right and the far left from their allies and coming through the center with a compromise bill. It was a legislative achievement that would not have been possible at that point without a Republican President. Had there been a Democrat in the White House, his recommendations to Congress would have been treated as pure political propaganda. It made a tremendous difference to have the original recommendation come from Eisenhower, to be embraced by Democrats, and put through the legislative mill in a serious vein. That converted the issue into a legislative *problem* and legislative problems can always be solved. Before that, it had been a political *cause* and political causes are *never* solved until they reach the problem stage.

The crucial significance of the civil rights bill was obscured by the passions of the times. It did not—as could no law—secure justice for all Americans and solve the problems that had been created by centuries of bigotry. But it did open the channels of American government to a tenth of the population for which all legislative doors had been slammed shut since 1875 (and for whom the doors had been only slightly ajar for the preceding decade). This meant that laws *could* be passed that would do whatever was possible legally. The impact of this upon people who previously had been denied participation in the institutions that ruled over them was extraordinary. True equality was still far away but at least the path could be seen.

The other significance of the bill was that it removed the bars to a Lyndon Johnson Presidential bid. Civil rights advocates thought it was too mild to accomplish any purpose. But they could not get past the fact that no one else had been able to pass *anything* for seventy-seven years. They could no longer claim that he was anti–civil rights; merely that he was not "strong enough" on the issue. Such arguments were not sufficiently convincing to rule him totally out of consideration. There was another side to this triumph, however, The fact that barriers had been removed to an LBJ White House drive also meant that he was to be regarded as a candidate for the office— no matter what he said. This had little impact upon his performance as floor leader in 1957 and 1958. But it was one of the major reasons for the poor performance in 1959 and 1960. His new status may have strengthened the support of the Southern bloc for him. But it cost in Northern support.

The Civil Rights Act broke a log jam that had been accumulating for decades. But once the jam was broken, it followed the classic patterns of legislation. In effect, the President sent Congress a proposal; Congress took the proposal and modified it; the measure was returned to the President and he signed it. The National Aeronautics and Space Act was not in that pattern. It represented one of the few instances in modern tmes where Congress took the initiative and the final outcome included a modification suggested by the President. The circumstances are so unusual that it is worthwhile to give them careful analysis.

The first time that Americans became aware of the potentialities of outer space was when the Soviet Union placed a satellite—known as sputnik—into orbit around the earth in October 1957. The Russians followed through in less than a month with a second satellite, carrying a dog in orbit (the satellite was dubbed Muttnik by the American press). The first had been something of a curiosity. The presence of a living animal made a distinct difference. In ordinary conversation, people began to speculate on what would happen when the satellites began to carry human beings who could presumably spy upon the United States from altitudes too great to reach with anti-aircraft.

There had been some preliminary foreshadowing of the onset of the Space Age, including a White House announcement a number of years earlier that an effort would be made to place in orbit a satellite about the size and shape of a basketball. There had also been considerable work in the armed services on intercontinental ballistics missiles, which required heavy rockets to lift them out of the earth's atmosphere. But the first announcement had not been sufficiently dramatic to attract attention and the work on the missiles had been cloaked by secrecy. The Soviet announcements of success in outer space produced the kind of shock that invariably follows surprise. It was as though some Cossack had leaped out of a doorway and shouted "boo" at a lone person walking down the street in the dark.

There were two clearly discernible elements in the public reaction. First, it meant to most Americans that our country had been outstripped in technology by the Soviet Union—a shattering blow to national pride. Second, it meant to most Americans that the Soviet Union could control the space around the earth and might be expected, as a hostile power, to use it to our harm. Neither prospect was welcome. Obviously, the American people needed a reliable assessment of what the situation really meant. They also needed an indication that the top levels of government were on top of the situation and ready to take action. Neither the assessment nor the indication were forthcoming.

The Eisenhower administration had correctly gauged

the temper of the American people on most issues up to this point. But no one in the White House grasped the political impact that accompanied the outer space technology. As Johnson stepped up his activity on the question, the administration actually made the classic mistake of pooh-poohing what was happening. President Eisenhower was quoted as saying that "Lyndon Johnson can keep his head in the stars; I am going to keep my feet on the ground," and his top assistant—Sherman Adams—referred scornfully to "outer space basketball." The President did not realize it but this was an instance in which he allowed power to slip from his fingers. He lost control of the issue and, in the end, was able to force only minor changes in the bill.

Johnson himself did not grasp the full impact either in the early days. He was bedeviled into taking a closer look at it by his staff, however, and realized immediately the potency of a well-organized campaign to step up the American effort. Fortunately for him, he also had a legislative vehicle for the campaign. It was the Senate Preparedness Subcommittee of the Senate Armed Services Committee. This had been the group that was formed under his sponsorship during the Korean War. It had conducted a number of investigations that brought him to favorable, although limited, public attention and had actually been moribund since he had become the Senate leader. He had kept it alive legally through the same instinct that causes people to store obsolete furniture in an attic rather than throw it into the trash.

Together with Russell, chairman of the Senate Armed Services Committee, Johnson attended a special briefing by the Armed Services in the Pentagon. The three services presented briefings on their progress in developing missiles and it was obvious that the United States was in reasonably good shape on this phase of outer space exploration. However, their concentration was almost entirely on missiles even though they were using individual scientists who were looking into other aspects of the new dimension that was opening up. The indications at this session were that an outside agency would be needed to launch vigorous studies into the science of outer space and also to give some coordination to the work that had begun already under the Army, the Air Force, and the Navy. They were too busy sniping at each other to do it themselves.

Upon the basis of the briefing, Russell, as chairman of the full committee, requested Johnson, as chairman of the subcommittee, to launch an investigation of the whole issue. The race was on.

The Preparedness Subcommittee was reactivated with staff from the Senate Democratic Policy Committee. An old Johnson friend—Edwin Weisl, a top New York lawyer with connections to the Hearst Corporation, the movie industry, and the Lehman brothers—was engaged as counsel. He brought with him top legal talent from his firm, Simpson, Thatcher and Bartlett, who mapped out one of the most dramatic sets of hearings ever held on a topic other than crime or scandal. It opened with testimony from Edward Teller, the so-called father of the hydrogen bomb. Drawing from his rich imagination, Teller painted a verbal picture of a universe in which mastery of outer space meant mastery of the world. The message he sent was clear. The Soviet Union had taken the first step into the heavens and unless we hurried to catch up, the later steps would find us under communist domination.

No succeeding witness was as dramatic. But Teller had supplied enough color for weeks of hearings. Factual data on the nature of the problems in outer space, which would have been dull under other circumstances, were followed avidly by the nation. Unfortunately, most of the "expert" testimony was being interpreted by lay politicians to whom physics was something taken after too much indulgence in pushcart pizza. The aim was to be spectacular and this was not at all hard to be when the subject matter was the whole universe and how to control it. In retrospect, some of the material should have been examined more carefully before being spread on the record in ex parte proceedings. One of the results was the public creation of a "missile gap"—a concept that we were almost hopelessly behind the Soviets in the possession of intercontinental ballistics missiles. The plugging of this gap became a campaign plank in John F. Kennedy's Presidential race of 1960 and it was rather embarrassing for him to discover, after his election, that it did not actually exist.

The genesis of the "missile gap" had been some closed hearings held by the Preparedness Subcommittee in which the Defense Department had presented a gloomy picture. The charts showed the Soviet Union leading the United States in every category of inertially guided missiles, although our nation still had sufficient capacity in conventional aircraft to defend itself. Furthermore, according to the testimony, we had failed to develop rockets of sufficient thrust to put heavy payloads into orbit. Had the committee members or the staff been sufficiently sophisticated to ask a few of the right questions, the whole hearing could have taken on a different coloration. The estimates had been based on the assumption that the Soviet Union had manufactured all the ICBMs for which it had the industrial capacity. Actually, as it turned out, they had waited for the development of better weapons and, if anything, they lagged behind us. As for the lesser thrust of our rockets, that problem was solved easily by hitching three of our rocket engines together. The charges of a "gap" were made in good faith but not with full knowledge.

Presiding over the hearings gave Lyndon Johnson almost a godlike aura in the press. He opened the year by making a speech before the Senate Democratic caucus that could easily have been set by a master musician to the notes of *Götterdämmerung*. One of the haunting lines spoke of outer space as the realm that might not present "the ultimate weapon" but would certainly present "the ultimate position." In its original form, it was a belligerent speech that seemed to signal an extension of the cold war with the Soviet Union into the regions beyond the earth's orbit. Had it been left in its original form, LBJ would have been labeled a warmonger—something the public would have approved at the time but which would have worked against him in the long run. Some of his Senate colleagues protested privately and quietly and he retrieved the situation by embracing a proposal to put the whole thing into the United Nations. This led to his being selected to present the U.S. Resolution on Outer Space to the United Nations itself. It was a moment when he stood at the very apex of the American political structure.

In the early spring, Johnson began to lose interest in the outer space issue. The public had begun to calm down and the Buck Rogers serials had played themselves out. He had never been comfortable with the subject matter and welcomed the rise of a new issue that he really understood—unemployment. A fairly serious recession had set in and, again, there had been little or no reaction from the White House. This left a leadership vacuum that the Senate, under the LBJ leadership, hastened to fill. This was a populist seventh heaven, passing housing bills, highway construction measures, and new public works projects. Had 1958 been a Presidential election year, the nation's next Chief Executive would have been a Texan.

The outer space issue was left dangling and, in retrospect, that might have been the best way to dispose of it. Some of his staff members, however, recognized that leaving it in limbo would ultimately work against Johnson. He had something of a reputation of exploiting issues without bringing them to a head and to forget outer space after all the drama would have been deadly. His staff had the National Aeronautics and Space Act drafted and presented it to him with a speech. He went through the motions and the bill eventually became law. During the course of the deliberations, Eisenhower, for the first time, expressed interest in the measure. Among other things, it proposed the creation of a council to advise the President. Ike insisted that the law should designate the President as its chairman. It did not seem very logical to appoint the President head of a group whose purpose was to give the President advice from the outside. But it was a cheap price to pay for the President's signature and his request was granted. When John F. Kennedy became President, one of his first requests to Congress was to designate the Vice President as chairman—a request that was also granted.

The Congress of 1957–1958 was one of the only two in

my experience—the other being the Eightieth Congress of 1947–1948—in which political leadership of the nation was assumed by the legislative branch of the government. It is interesting to speculate on how and why it happened. In 1947 and 1948, of course, the Congress was Republican controlled and on a conservative tack. In 1957 and 1958, the Congress was Democratic controlled and on a liberal-populist tack. But when one probes more deeply than the party labels, it becomes apparent that the two bodies—separated by all the issues that had accumulated during the ten-year interval—were characterized by more similarities than differences. In both instances, control was in the hands of what was technically the President's opposition. In both instances, Presidential initiatives in the field of foreign policy received sympathetic and favorable welcomes. In both instances, the domestic initiatives seized by the Congressional leaders were in areas where there was a vacuum of Executive leadership. And in both instances, the period of legislative control was followed by a period of legislative inability to act. This is not altogether clear if one considers only the elections in the fall of 1958, which returned huge Democratic majorities in both the House and the Senate. But it becomes clear when one looks at the total ineffectiveness of those majorities in the 1959–1960 Congress. It is obvious that legislative leadership of the nation is something of a freak, whatever the Founding Fathers may have intended. Some further reflections on this question will follow in the next chapter.

The last two years of the Congressional decade can only be described as dreary. The huge Democratic majorities turned out to be unwieldy and a revivified Eisenhower used his veto power to make clear who was boss. A seemingly interminable debate on amendments to strengthen the Civil Rights Act was finally brought to a conclusion by the application of a few face-savers and the glorious rush of legislation that had prevailed in the previous Congresses was stopped dead in its tracks. The forthcoming Presidential election in which Eisenhower could *not* run set the character of legislative activity.

On the Democratic side of the aisle, there were simply too many candidates. No one doubted Kennedy's commanding lead. He had been working on nothing else for four years. But neither did anyone doubt that Johnson would show up at the convention with a sackful of delegates. Most of them would be from the South but there was a good chance that he would pick up others from the West and the Border States. There was every prospect for a deadlocked convention and this encouraged more than one individual to hope that the result would be for lightning to strike. The major prospects were Senator Stuart Symington of Missouri and Henry L. "Scoop" Jackson of Washington.

The Republicans did not have the same problem. It was obvious that their candidate would be Richard M. Nixon. His party was not particularly happy with the choice. He was too far to the internationalist side for the GOP right wing; had played the communist hunt game too zealously for the GOP liberals. But both had become disorganized during the Eisenhower years. The Republican liberals had become diluted by the defection of some members, such as Wayne Morse, and by the rise of the Democratic Party in New England, which had been the GOP Yankee individualist stronghold. The Republican right had put too many eggs in the anti-communist basket and found itself without a moving issue when the "Red Scare" died down. It was some time before the conservatives discovered other issues such as abortion and school prayer and economic fundamentalism. There was simply no solid base from which to launch an anti-Nixon counteroffensive.

To complicate the situation still further, it became obvious to his close associates that Johnson's interest in the Senate leadership had waned. This was not necessarily traceable to Presidential ambitions. His intimates realized that he was going through some personal crises that made him blow hot and blow cold—alternately and often on the same day—on a White House bid. The result was a grossly inept Presidental campaign and a just as inept Senate leadership.

There was one other factor, however, that must be taken into account. The first six years of the Johnson era had taken place because there were a number of problems to be solved and a national consensus willing to solve them. The housing, health, and civil rights measures that had been passed did not solve the problems, although they did make some dents. But even though they did not solve the problems, they exhausted the consensus that made the measures possible. Coupled with the approaching change in the White House, it was enough to bring the possibilities of legislative action to an end. The curtain was down.

13
What Price Efficiency?

Among those who have been close to the Senate, there is a distinct air of nostalgia when they contemplate the decade of the fifties. The reasons are obvious. This is an era that places a very high value on production efficiency and, by that standard, it was certainly the most productive Senate since the first two years of the New Deal. Legislation poured out of the mill in what seemed to be tidal waves and some of it—such as civil rights—represented issues that had been kept at a standstill for decades. Furthermore, some of it—such as the Outer Space Act—could be termed "creative" (a buzzword of modern industry) in that it launched new approaches independently of the executive branch of the government.

Because of the respect accorded to the Senate of the fifties, it is well to review its history, as I have sought to do in this book. What emerges from such a review in my mind is that it was successful because the conditions of the times held out prospects for success to shrewd leadership. The important matter is not the specific history but what that specific history teaches us as to the role of the Senate and how it works. Basically, it is the organ of orderly change in our society that allows the shifts that are needed to meet new circumstances but controls those shifts so they do not get ahead of the willingness of the American people to accept them.

The Senate has always been a pet target of the reformers because of its exasperating slowness. Those attacks are even more widespread in a management-oriented age when "efficiency" is the watchword of our society. When it comes to production, efficiency is a goal to be cherished. But when it comes to passing laws, production efficiency can be disastrous. It is too bad the phrase was ever invented.

As leader, Lyndon Johnson was thoroughly aware of the value of a display of "efficiency." One of my most thoroughly detested chores was that of preparing a list of 100 "major" bills that had been passed during the course of a session. These would be included in a final speech that impressed everyone but me and Richard B. Russell. It sounds like a relatively easy list to compile. But the reality of Senate life is that most of the important legislation falls within an area of executive-legislative agreement and consists of continuing authority to keep the government operating. Any session that approves more than five or six truly ground-breaking bills is meeting under extraordinary circumstances. The result was that I had to exert a considerable amount of imagination to reach the required number. One year, I was so desperate that I had to include a routine measure to require federal inspection of poultry. It did not solve any real problem, as all the states had adequate inspection laws already. Still, it made the list of the hundred greatest that year—and was promptly dubbed the "chicken feed" bill by the press, which was highly amused by the whole performance.

From a public relations standpoint, Johnson was absolutely correct. For me, however, there was something wrong in equating the few really major bills—civil rights; outer space; housing and health acts—with ordinary legislative activities. I also agreed with Russell that the lists were piling up troubles for future Senates. What was going to be the public reaction during periods when the political climate of the country was not favorable to "productivity"? That is the crux of the matter. Under our system, there are times when the Congress, and especially the Senate, *must* play an obstructive role in order to discharge its responsibilities. What happens then if our people have been educated to the belief that legislative output is the sole criterion for judgment?

I do not believe it is possible to participate in the life of the Senate for any length of time without becoming aware of the fallacy of the productivity standard. Quite a long list of political science interns were assigned to my office and it was fascinating to observe the change in their attitudes. One of them said to me, when he left: "I came here with all sorts of ideas as to what Senators should do to step up passage of bills. I now realize that when they come here, there are certain things that they must do and I am revising all my thinking." It is now becoming more widely agreed that the function of the Congress as a whole is to resolve political differences in the nation and that the specific function of the Senate is to provide the longer-term view in that resolution.

The function of resolving political differences automatically requires a standard other than productivity. It is entirely possible to ignore political problems when policy has been set and the only objective of a governmental institution is to handle economic and social questions. Then, the productivity standard is quite valid. But the resolution of political differences requires a climate within the nation that makes the resolution possible. Congress cannot really resolve such issues for us. It can only lead us to a solution. And when the elements of consensus are not present, it cannot lead us anywhere. It can only resort to the educational process of the public dialogue in the hope that the people will eventually be brought to a point of reason.

This is the point at which so many people become impatient with democracy. There are times when legislative action is simply impossible—no matter how urgent the occasion. To conceive of a civil rights bill at any time from 1875 to 1950 was to dream an idle dream. To array the United States against the Fascist powers in the early and mid-thirties (when it required legislation) could be nothing but a hope on the part of a few Americans who were looked upon by their fellow countrymen as suspicious "internationalists." There was no agreement for either action within the United States and this meant that there could be no agreement within the Congress itself.

Here we come across one of the reasons why the Presidency seems to shine so brightly in contrast with the Congress. The President *can* act—to a limited extent—in the absence of a political consensus. At the very least, he can throw the prestige of the White House into the public dialogue as Franklin Delano Roosevelt, acting through his wife, did when legislative achievement in the field of civil rights was not in the cards. He can go further than that, as FDR did when he set up a voluntary FEPC (Fair Employment Practice Commission) to help blacks get jobs during World War II. If the necessary action is in the international field, the President can go even further. He can make commitments that may not be as binding as formal treaties but that will nevertheless nudge the United States into irretrievable courses. FDR, for example, did not need Congressional approval to escort munitions ships halfway across the Atlantic to Great Britain. The act itself, however, made further intervention virtually inevitable.

There is one other governmental institution that can act without a political consensus and that can, in fact, go much further than the President. It is the court system of the nation that can hand down sweeping verdicts that profoundly affect the lives of every American but that will have behind them no legislative mandate whatsoever. The Presidential office, after all, is partly political and partly non-political, which means the Chief Executive can go only partway in acting without popular approval. But the Supreme Court is, in theory, totally non-political and can provide us, as a result, with a safety valve when action is absolutely imperative and legislative action is blocked. The decisions of the Supreme Court in regard to the integration of the public schools are a case in point. They were handed down far in advance of the Civil Rights Act of 1957.

The Presidential and judicial powers can never accomplish a fully satisfactory resolution of problems. At best, they can buy time until a legislative solution—which means a political solution—is forthcoming. However, the exercise of those powers paints a picture in which Congress suffers. Alongside of its more flexible and "efficient" brother branches of government, it is bound to look poor. Usually, it cannot even put its prestige behind a solution to an issue because Congress can commit itself only through its votes. If it could cast a "prestige" vote, it could cast a substantive vote. When all these factors are taken together, it is little wonder that so much of the modern analysis of government in the United States centers upon devices to make the legislative branch of our government more efficient. The Senate bears the brunt of this concern simply because it lacks the machinery by which issues *can* be brought to a vote in the House of Representatives when the leadership is really determined.

There is no question but that the Senate can be exasperating. The untrammeled right of free speech in that body is most likely to be exercised by those whose oratorical gifts leave something to be desired. A filibuster, even when one is in agreement with the effort to block the bill under discussion, is a disheartening spectacle. The committee procedures that can keep legislation pigeonholed for months are not calculated to soothe the nerves of the impatient. And when, on top of this, it develops that a substantial majority is sometimes not enough to get a bill enacted into law, it is little wonder that the Senate is the target for most of the reform movements.

Most of the apologists for the Senate make the mistake of accepting the reformist assumptions. The unlimited speech is characterized as essential to determine the merits of legislation. The filibuster is described as something that happens only occasionally and must be tolerated as a price for assuring thoroughness of consideration. The committee procedures are looked upon as merely a legislative device that is necessary for efficiency but that is bound to slip up occasionally. These responses are all nonsense. The merits of a bill are thoroughly covered in the committee reports. The long-winded speeches are intended only to impress constituents (except for the sponsor, who usually tries to make a legislative record for future court interpretation). The bills get lost in committee pigeonholes only when the leadership wants them lost. The real question is not whether there is a need for these delaying devices in order to secure "good" laws. The real question is whether the Senate should have some extraordinary procedures to delay legislation even when a majority of the Senate is in favor of it.

To find an answer to this question, it might be well to go back to the Constitutional Convention and look at the circumstances that impelled the Founding Fathers to establish the institution in the first place. Fundamentally, it was a question of holding the Union together. The smaller states were disturbed by the idea of a national legislature representing population only. They saw themselves powerless to secure laws they needed against the opposition of the larger states. The response was to establish the Senate with a pledge written into the Constitution itself that every state would have equal representation in it forever. The legal validity of such a promise is somewhat dubious. But the concept has justified itself over and over again. The Senate, with its independence from population pressures, has proven to be the friend of the smaller states right up to modern times. What has been less noticed is that it has also played an important role in sustaining national unity. There are times when issues should be allowed to simmer. The Senate frequently keeps them simmering despite all pressures to bring them to a head.

The Senate is often accused of violating the concept of majority rule in the United States. The problem, if one examines the accusation with care, is that it does not delve very deeply into the questions of what is meant by "majority" and what is meant by "majority rule." The latter is the easiest to consider. The Senate does *not* prevent the majority from ruling; it merely prevents the majority from doing everything that it wants to do when it wants to do it. The Senate does not grant the minority the right to rule. It merely grants the minority the right to block legislation until it has been demonstrated that there is a clearcut, consistent majority behind it and until it is apparent that the minority is willing to remain within the community when it is forced to give in to legislation that it considers abhorrent.

The issue of what constitutes a majority is somewhat more complex. Actually, there is no such thing as a majority in the United States on any unresolved issue. What we are really dealing with is a series of shifting blocs, which, from time to time, find it possible to build temporary coalitions that are capable of action along limited lines. This describes what John Calhoun—a brilliant analyst despite his bigotry—referred to as "the concurrent majority." The Senate is held together solely by a set of specific issues; it is not characterized by loyalty to the coalition (only to the issues) by the members of the various blocs; and its constituent elements invariably approach the struggle with

197

varying degrees of enthusiasm, as many of them have joined the coalition merely in trade for support on something in which they are really interested.

In the last analysis, we must always come back to a simple question. Is there a value to the dilatory practices of a democracy or do we put up with them because they are a price of freedom? The temper of our times is one that holds that there is *no* value to delay in action beyond the time required for prudent men to find the best solutions to problems. The world is said to have become too complex to permit the "luxury" of extended debate under the shadow of the atomic bomb and the intercontinental ballistic missile. This argument can be made very compelling when we consider that a missile fired from the Soviet Union could destroy New York or Chicago in about half an hour.

These arguments would be even more compelling if the "efficient" people had a better track record. Twice in this century we have bypassed the dilatory practices of the Constitution to plunge into major actions. Once was in Korea; the second was in Vietnam. In neither case were the issues submitted to Congress for determination prior to the act. In neither case can it be said with any validity that the legislative branch of the government interfered with the conduct of those two major wars. The outcome was that one was fought to a stalemate and one was fought to a disastrous defeat. But what was even more important is the strain that they put upon our society. A whole generation of young people was "turned off" by Vietnam and defiance of the government became the respectable stance for American youth. One wonders what would be the result if another war had come along before the disillusionment began to fade. Everyone who spent any time on the college campuses during Vietnam was forced to realize that the basic fabric of our society was threatened.

The intellectual currents of modern times do not delve very deeply into the question of holding nations together. Generally, it is taken for granted that they will remain intact unless overthrown by an outside force. Therefore the tendency is to concentrate on the processes for problem solving. The Congress of the United States does not shine very brightly in such circumstances.

Do we really want "efficient" Congresses? The answer is a flat no if we equate efficiency with legislative production. We can live with it in such periods as the fifties (which I have been covering in this book) because there had been so many barren years in which unresolved issues had piled up. But on a yearly basis, it would keep the executive branch in a constant state of turmoil and saddle our people with long lists of laws that they really did not want.

Lyndon B. Johnson illustrated the problems that would arise during his first two years as President. There were a series of circumstances that made Congress all too willing to follow his lead (not the least of which were his appeals to pass laws as a monument to a martyred President). He himself had more legislative skill than any other man who ever entered the White House. The result was an outpouring of legislation that gave the appearance of a veritable revolution in American life. Actually, very little was *done* because the Executive agencies were not given a breathing space to organize themselves and because Vietnam absorbed so much government money there was little left for the social programs. I have vivid memories of an assistant calling me after I had left the White House with the news that the President had ordered a doubling of one of his more popular programs for slum children (Head Start) and had not noticed there was no money for the doubling in the budget. This one was solved—it was relatively cheap. But most of the shortfalls were *not* resolved. The "Great Society" was a victim of too much legislative action and too little Executive action. The President's reach exceeded his grasp; and Congress went along with the reach.

The results were not at all fortunate. The scores of headlines on the passage of social legislation created the impression that the entire government was devoted to uplifting the ghettoes and that everything else was secondary. The stark reality was that life changed very little for the men and women at the bottom of the ladder—leaving many of them with the suspicion that they were victims of a razzle-dazzle con game. I am convinced that the riots that broke out in Los Angeles, Detroit, and Washington, D.C., and other cities in 1968 were the outcome of frustrated expectations. To many of the "whites" outside the ghettoes, however, they looked like the repayment of favors with ingratitude. A far, far better thing it would have been had the Congress delayed passage of many of the bills until they had been thoroughly debated and *until they could be funded*. From such efficiency as was demonstrated, good Lord deliver us!

None of this can be—or should be—taken to mean that the dilatory processes will bring us the "best solution" in the sense that there is a "right" and a "wrong" answer to every quadratic equation. Collective intelligence is not necessarily better than individual intelligence (although it frequently is) just as "man-in-the-street" wisdom is not necessarily better than expert opinion (although it frequently is). However, in the governing process it is not enough for a solution to be logical and factually based. It must also be acceptable to the public. The acceptance need not be enthusiastic. It can even be reluctant and grudging. But it must be based on the feeling that all sides were heard and the minorities were not totally disregarded.

The House of Representatives is the body that is the most likely to reflect current opinion at any given moment. But were it the only legislative arm, we would be in trouble quickly. The House reacts too fast. It is an excellent spur to action. But the members are too close to the next election to ride out popular storms. The Senate is the body that is the best barometer for deciding when a coalition on an issue is truly stable and action is possible. I hope we leave it alone. We need it!

14

The Center
Cannot Hold

This book was made possible because my editor believed that an examination of the Senate of the 1950s could shed some light on our legislative problems today. The one point that can be made with certainty is that the 1950s Senate worked and the 1980s Senate is, at best, a somewhat careless caretaker of the Congressional heritage. It even went so far as to abdicate a basic responsibility of the whole Congress when, together with the House, it turned over to faceless, bureaucratic technicians the job of determining the governmental programs that will be cut. *Sic transit gloria!* This is the first step on a path that has grave, disquieting implications for the future of our divided-powers democracy. Will the computer conquer all?

Basically, what I have done here is to relive that portion

of my Washington life that I remember most fondly. I have not done so merely for the sake of nostalgia. As I have been writing, I have been seeking clues as to what was done right then that is not being done right now. The search has not been an easy one. First, times have changed. The issues of the fifties are not the issues of the eighties and the society in which we live today is a far cry from that in which we lived then. Second, I no longer have access to the Senate on a daily basis and must confine my observations of it to long-distance views. This means that I must draw some inferences that do not have the benefit of the direct contact I once had. Nevertheless, looking at what I have written and contrasting it with what I read in the daily press, it is possible to draw some conclusions with a reasonable degree of confidence—at least on what is wrong. What to do about it is another question.

First, it is obvious that many of the circumstances that made the 1950s Senate such a productive body no longer exist. That was a decade in which we felt no budget crunch. It was an age of optimism. We had plenty of money (or we thought we had plenty of money) and we wanted to use it to expand. As long as the expansion was kept within sensible limits, we were willing to go along with it—even into outer space. Second, we had a centrist President who was rather conservative but perfectly willing to be indulgent in signing "reasonably" liberal bills as long as the people who sponsored those bills protected his foreign policy. Third, the major issues were controllable (civil rights and foreign policy) because their time had come and sensible men knew how to carry them for the final mile.

Only President Reagan can say that this is an age of optimism in which we are facing the future with confidence. His capacity to say—and obviously believe—what is not there has an undeniable charm that may account for his popularity. The fact remains that this is an age of apprehension in which the spirit is to "hang on" if possible but to be resigned to the very real possibility of falling off life's merry-go-round. On every side, the battle is not to expand but to cut losses and we feel now—as we did not feel in the fifties—that we exist in a universe of limited resources. As any college professor who listens to his students knows, they graduate in the hope they can find a niche in the economic machinery. They no longer think that the world is their oyster.

Furthermore, we do not have a centrist President, although I doubt whether he is quite as conservative as his rhetoric. Instead we have a Chief Executive who is dedicated to the proposition that we must cut back government everywhere except in the field of defense. He has no desire to play the kind of games with Congress that were played by his illustrious predecessor nor does he give the legislative branch the "hooks" that were proffered by Eisenhower. Ike, at the very least, sent messages that carried within themselves room for interpretation. They could be read with equal validity by liberal eyes and by conservative eyes and could come out two different ways. Mr. Reagan leaves little room for doubt.

As for *the* major issue of the day, it is almost impossible to control budget cutting by normal, political means. Over the years, constituencies have developed for all the governmental programs and to cut them back now is to produce major dislocations in our society. This is so obvious that no one is even arguing against cuts. The battle is over the areas where the greatest cuts should be made—defense or social services. In such a contest, the President's power of the initiative is an enormous asset. He is the one who starts the ball rolling and those who are not in sympathy with him find themselves continually reacting, which is always the weakest side of the debate. It is not advantageous strategically to be continually on the defensive.

This, to me, raises one of the most crucial of all the differences between the two Congressional periods. What I find lacking in the modern Senate is the art of pitting the left and the right against each other and coming through the middle. This was the strategic base upon which the Democratic leadership of the fifties operated. The left could be depended upon to cancel out the right and the right could be counted on to cancel out the left. While the two factions were fighting each other, the centrists could hammer out something viable. This was the formula that produced the Civil Rights Act and guided the legislative battlers through the outpouring of social legislation.

There are many forces working against such a strategy at the present time. The Eisenhower messages set up an agenda that provided elbowroom for all sides. Mr. Reagan leaves no choice but to be for or against him. He forces the hard, sharp confrontations that always put Congress at a disadvantage. The strength of the legislative branch in a divided-powers system of government is its capacity to take legislation apart in detail and put it back together again in myriad, subtle ways. The strength of the Presidency is its capacity to be always first on the draw with the heaviest firepower when the scenario has been adapted from "Showdown at the OK Corral." Mr. Reagan, very wisely, keeps the disputation on his strongest level.

Mr. Reagan is also very good at setting up legislative agendas that weaken the opposition by diverting its strength to secondary battles. There is no doubt in my mind that he is constantly pushing forward proposals to abolish abortion and permit prayer in the public schools for precisely that reason. It is unlikely that anything is going to happen to either idea. The American system is far too complex to permit action on such measures unless there is a really strong consensus in their favor. I find no such consensus and neither can anyone else except those who are so enamored with the proposals that they only see what they want to see. Nevertheless, they put heart in the conservatives, who are a bit suspicious of Mr. Reagan's status as a true believer, and they push the liberals into expending their energies on debates that are essentially hot air.

Under these circumstances, the liberal wing of the Senate has virtually abdicated its historic role. It is no longer a central point for *public* debate over positive proposals to cure the ills of society. It may well be hatching ideas in the privacy of suites in the Senate Office Building. But those ideas certainly do not penetrate as far as Milwaukee. The communications I receive from my liberal friends (mostly appeals for money to offset the conservative political war chest being raised by Jesse Helms) are entirely defensive. They ask me to support them because they are *against* conservative proposals to abolish abortion on demand; because they are *against* prayers in the public schools; because they are *against* cutting social services from the federal budget. They are fighting a rearguard action and their communications have a tone of panic.

A defensive liberalism does not play a constructive role in the public dialogue. It deprives the nation of a fundamental need—a constant churning of new proposals and original concepts. The center, of course, will have the final word, which is as it should be. But it is not in the nature of the center to explore or promote new paths. Left to its own devices, without the constant prodding of the two ends of the political spectrum, the center will leave things alone. It is not an innovative force in our society.

It is unlikely that there will be an upsurge in liberal thought in the foreseeable future. Innovation requires a dedication of resources and this is an era of retrenchment rather than advance. The concept of throwing money at a problem to drive it away is not very tasteful to people anymore. But no one has discovered solutions that can be bought "on the cheap." Until such solutions are discovered, there will not be much of a constituency for the liberals.

On the other side of the spectrum, the conservatives have dedicated themselves to an impossible goal. They are literally trying to demolish the elaborate social welfare structure that has been built up since 1932. Whether they are right or wrong in some Platonic sense is irrelevant to what will happen. Our society has adjusted itself to that structure and the social dislocations that will follow the demolition are more than sensible men and women will allow.

The basic point is that the "debate" going on at the present time is unlikely to produce dynamic solutions. The overall picture is one of conservatives embarked on an offensive that they cannot win and liberals confining themselves to slowing down whatever conservative gains can be made. There are real arguments in the field of foreign policy but these are not the kind that will lead to profound changes in our society. The Senate—and, for that matter, the Congress as a whole—is not coming to grips with the fantastic changes that are taking place in America. Until they do, no amount of Senate reorganization and no amount of prodding is going to change the picture.

What is so strange about this situation is that our society *is* going through profound mutations that have the capacity to produce not only a new way of life but a new type of human being. These are being accepted virtually without comment because our political leaders have not found methods of handling them as issues. The most prominent is the rapidly increasing trend toward amalgamation of government and business. There is a certain irony here. The government itself is engaged in activities that are certain to alter the whole shape of America. But these activities are being discussed only in terms of whether they will be a success or a failure.

There have, of course, always been connections between government and business in any nation where business existed. In the age of mercantilism, governments thought it proper to set up conditions that favored home industry and sometimes set up lucrative opportunities for favorites of the ruling powers. Businessmen have been known to corrupt public officials and public officials have been known to solicit corruption. In all of these instances, however, there was a clear-cut separation between the two. Governments might foster industrial enterprises and political leaders might feather their nests through it. They did not mix corporate management and government except to the extent that some regulations were needed to prevent fraud. They were distinct sectors of our society divided by lines that were not crossed.

For a number of years, those lines have been breaking down—imperceptibly, at first, but emerging into the open so smoothly that the process was not recognized as a phenomenon. It probably began with the farm programs in which the government tried to regulate the marketplace and, in doing so, began to buy and sell commodities on a massive basis. The necessity of controlling production during World War II inured us to the presence of the government in our daily economic life on a scale that had never been known before. However, it was still regulatory as were the export controls that were established during the cold war with the Soviet Union. Today we have gone even further as the government has stepped in to prevent huge corporations from going bankrupt. Lockheed and Chrysler are only forerunners of what lies ahead. The merger of government and industry is an inevitable result of bigness. We cannot allow the failure of the giant corporations of present times because such failure would be too disruptive to our society.

Equally intriguing is the drive of state governments to bring specific industries into their territories. At the present time, the government of Wisconsin—the state in which I live—is offering package deals to the American Motors Company to locate its principal facilities here. The terms under discussion go pretty far—not only favorable tax treatment but actual help in the construction of new facilities. To top the whole thing off, two other states are bidding for the corporation with the same zeal. It is a bitter battle with very high stakes. The winner can bring home jobs and revenue-generating activity that will not come if the Governor keeps his hands off the development of industry.

It is idle to think in terms of reversing the trend. The conservatives talk of reducing the size of the U.S. Government and returning to a free market. They do have the capacity to reduce the size of the government. Unfortunately for their thesis, however, they have achieved the capacity at a time when the "free market" is vanishing under the impact of economic merger. Bigness is the order of the day and the smaller the government is, the less ability it will have to cope with the huge conglomerates already in existence and those that are rapidly taking shape. Many Americans, especially around income tax time, would like to "get government off our backs." But they do not want to do so by replacing it with corporate riders who can be just as demanding as government and less accountable.

All of the signs point to the creation of a corporate state, an entity in which business and government will be indistinguishable. Lockheed and Chrysler were the precursors. Both were bail-out operations. But it is only a question of time until the natural forces of society will push government into earlier entries into the industrial field before corporations reach the bail-out stage. It will seem like a natural development. Already, people are looking hungrily at Lee Iacocca as a Presidential candidate because of his success in rescuing Chrysler, with governmental help, from a serious crash. I do not have the faintest idea whether he will eventually become President or even make a serious stab at it. But I do find intriguing the large-scale willingness to think of him as an occupant of the oval room in the White House. It has been a long time since a businessman has been a political hero.

On this question, I am only scratching the surface and I do not intend to go any further. I am not trying to analyze the current scene. I am only calling attention to the fact that the political dialogue is not delving into what is probably the most important social movement of our times. Until it does, I do not expect to see a very effective Senate or a very effective Congress, for that matter. Legislatures in the United States work well only when they are confronting real disputes. Perhaps that is just as well. It is probably useful to have political machinery that does not grind out laws when the public is not ready to receive them.

That may well be the most important lesson in reviewing the fifties. The Senate of that era had remarkably astute leadership and was remarkably productive in terms of an outpouring of social legislation. But the astute leadership was only a part of the story. The other part was a public that was *ready* for such an outpouring. The major reason for the readiness was simply that every issue had been chewed over and talked through before it came anywhere near the Senate floor. In addition, there was a balance between the two ends of the political spectrum that made sensible approaches possible.

There is no public ready for solutions today because no one has sparked a dialogue on the issues. On our social welfare legislation, we are talking about the past and how much of it should be preserved and how much should go by the board. On the moral issues of abortion and school prayer, we are talking about things that are highly unlikely to happen. And on foreign policy, we are talking about new sets of facts but not new approaches. This is not the stuff of which great legislatures are made.

The continuing growth of our society has raised our social institutions to unprecedented levels of bigness. We are faced with the necessity of deciding whether the older forms of economic control are sufficient. Left to themselves, there is little doubt as to what will happen. We have developed combinations that not only threaten monopoly in some areas of economic endeavor but open prospects of monopoly over a wide range of industrial activity. The Textron Corporation, for example, manufactures helicopters, fountain pens, staplers, foundry products, and just about everything else except textiles. Yet, it is far from the largest conglomerate. The diversity of the corporations put together by the late Howard Hughes is absolutely awe-inspiring. And it is difficult to find brand-name food products that do not have some connection with General Mills or General Foods. The whole trend of our times is toward centralization. Can it continue without either outstripping the powers of government or suffering intervention by the government in the form of active participation?

It takes time to develop political issues. We have not had that time—not even the time to develop a vocabulary. But what I am advancing here is the thesis that we are not going to have another "productive" Senate until after we have had a real dialogue on the real problems before us. The various proposals to reorganize the Senate are a waste of time.

I started this chapter on the basis of the William Butler

Yeats quote "The center cannot hold." In a very real sense it is not holding now because the two extremes of our society are not playing the essential roles of sparking the public dialogue. But another quote from the same poem may be more apropos. It is: "And what rough beast . . . Slouches towards Bethlehem to be born."

The answer to our problems is first to find out what we want. That is the function of national debate and the more quickly we turn to it, the more quickly our political organs will return to their normal role.

Acknowledgments

I would like to give appropriate recognition to Michael L. Gillette, Chief of Oral History Programs for the Lyndon B. Johnson Library, and to Regina Greenwell, Joan Kennedy, and Lesley Williams, members of his staff. Their painstaking compilation of materials from interviews and careful checking of the facts gave me not only an inspiration for this book but a rich data bank upon which I could draw. I also wish to express thanks to Bea Bourgeois who typed the manuscript under conditions of pressure that would stagger the hero or heroine of an aspirin commercial.

Index

abortion issue, 189, 206, 211–212
Acheson, Dean, 57, 136–137
Adams, Sherman, 182
agricultural legislation, 50, 153–158
Alexander, William H., 160–161
American Meat Institute (AMI), 155, 156
anti-Semitism, 72–73
arms embargo, 68–70
Arvey, Jacob M., 26, 176
Austin, Warren R., 101

Baker, Bobby, 41
Beeson, Lloyd, 131–133
Benson, Ezra Taft, 155–156
Borah, William, 65, 68, 69–70
Bricker, John W., 80–83
Bricker amendment, 80–84, 150
Bridges, Styles, 18
Brownell, Herbert, 103
budget issues, 204–205, 206–207
business-government amalgamation, 208–211

Byrd, Harry F., 109, 134
Byrnes, James, 114–115

Calhoun, John, 197
Cannon's Precedents in the House of Representatives, 43
Capehart, Homer, 108, 109, 110
Case, Francis, 167
"cash and carry" law, 68–70
Chiang Kai-shek, 51–52, 53–54, 76, 149
China, 51–52, 53–54, 57, 58, 75, 76
China lobby, 51–52
city political machines, 24–27, 29, 55, 61, 98, 115, 117, 118–119, 176
civil rights, 13, 19, 22, 31–32, 33, 48, 49–50, 73, 80, 90–91, 94, 106, 114–115, 118, 119–120, 121–124, 127, 129, 190, 193, 194, 203
Civil Rights Act (1957), 35, 36, 41, 46, 120, 127, 178–180, 188, 194, 205
Clark, Bennett Champ, 65

communist issue, domestic, 52–57, 75, 97, 135–139
Communist Party of the United States, 52, 56, 60
Connally, John, 170–171
Connally, Tom, 70
Costello, Frank, 25
Crump, Ed, 24, 26, 98

Daley, Richard, 26, 27, 176
Daniel, Price, 169
Davies, Aled, 155, 157
DePriest, Oscar, 118
Dewey, Thomas E., 48, 96, 102–103, 175–176
direct election constitutional amendment, 44
Dirksen, Everett, 173–174

education, 23, 73, 80, 147
Eisenhower, Dwight D., 27, 30, 32, 36, 48, 62–63, 74, 75, 76–78, 79, 80, 97, 101, 103, 104–105, 107, 108, 111–112, 125, 129, 130, 131, 137, 148,

Eisenhower (cont.)
149, 150, 151–152,
153, 155, 157–158,
159, 163, 164, 168,
173, 174, 175, 176–
177, 179, 181–182,
186, 187, 204, 205
Erwin, Sam, 144

Farley, Jim, 117
farm legislation, 50,
153–158
Fitzgerald, John J.
(Honey Fitz), 29
flexible price support
program, 155–158
foreign policy, 8–10,
51–54, 56–58, 64–84,
103–104, 130, 203,
208, 212
Franco, Francisco, 56

Galbraith, Arthur, Jr., 29
Genocide Convention,
U.N., 75–76, 79
George, Walter F., 83,
115
George amendment, 83
Gore, Albert, 172–173
government-business
amalgamation,
208–211
Greek-Turkish aid pro-
gram, 75

Haggerty, Jim, 103
Hague, Frank A., 26, 27,
119, 176
Harrison, Pat, 114
Hayden, Carl, 42, 143
health issues, 23, 73, 80,
147, 177
Helms, Jesse, 206
highway construction,
177, 186
Hiss, Alger, 22, 30, 52,
75, 136
Hope, Clifford, 154
housing legislation, 23,
73, 80, 107–110, 147,
177, 186, 189

Human Rights Cove-
nant, U.N., 75, 79, 82
Humphrey, Hubert H.,
4, 18, 19, 22, 32–35,
52, 98

Iacocca, Lee, 210–211
intercontinental ballistic
missiles (ICBMs), 181,
183, 184–185
internationalism, 64,
67–68, 69–71, 73–77,
188, 193
Interstate Commerce
Clause of the Constitu-
tion, 81
isolationism, 9, 51,
64–77, 78, 79, 80–84,
103–104, 158

Jackson, Henry (Scoop),
98, 188
Johnson, Edwin C., 87
Johnson, Hiram, 65
Johnson, Lyndon B., 4,
11, 12, 14, 15, 18, 22,
31, 33–34, 35–37,
39–40, 41, 45–46,
47–48, 63, 71, 78–79,
80, 88–89, 92, 93–94,
96, 97, 98, 99, 104–
105, 106–107, 109,
110–112, 127–128, 129,
130, 132–133, 135,
146, 148, 150, 159,
160, 164–168, 169–174,
175, 177–178, 179–180,
182–183, 185–186, 188,
189, 191, 199–200
jury trial, 41

Kefauver, Estes M.,
22–25, 27, 28, 35, 46,
93–94, 98, 111, 160,
162, 172, 173
Kelly, Ed, 26, 27, 119,
176
Kennedy, Edward M., 29
Kennedy, John F., 22,
27, 28–29, 37, 97–98,

160, 172, 173, 176,
184, 186, 188
Kennedy, Robert F., 29
Kerr, Robert S., 18, 134,
160–162
Knowland, William F.,
18, 79, 148–150, 173
Korean War, 14, 31, 48,
57–58, 63, 198–199
Kuchel, Thomas, 18

labor racketeering, 22,
28, 98
LaFollette, Robert M.,
Jr., 65
LaFollette-Monroney
Legislative Reorgani-
zation Act, 11–12
Lattimore, Owen, 136
Lawrence, Dave, 27
League of Nations, 66
Lend-Lease, 71
Long, Russell B., 134
Lucas, Scott W., 85
Luce, Henry, 52
Ludlow, Louis, 67
Lyndon B. Johnson, A Mem-
oir (Reedy), 143–144

MacArthur, Douglas,
14–15, 31, 58
McCarran, Pat, 42–43,
135
McCarthy, Joseph R.,
52, 135–139, 142–145,
148
McClellan, John L., 138
McFarland, Ernest W.,
85
McKellar, Kenneth, 114
McNary, Charles, 101
Mao Tse-tung, 75
Marshall, George C., 135
Marshall Plan, 75
medical care, 23, 73, 80,
147, 177
Milliken, Eugene, 18,
86–90
missile gap, 37, 184–
185

Index

Moley, Raymond, 118
Monroney, A. S. (Mike), 160–161
Morrison, Cameron, 141
Morse, Wayne, 188
NAACP, 34
National Aeronautics and Space Act, 151, 178, 180–186
natural gas bill, 46, 165–168
Neutrality Acts, 8–10, 67–71
New Deal, 54, 67–68, 73, 80, 103–104, 114, 115, 117, 178
Nixon, Richard M., 22, 29–31, 52, 97, 98, 188
North Atlantic Treaty Organization (NATO), 75
Nye, Gerald P., 67, 72

O'Brien, Lawrence F., 29
O'Donnell, Kenneth P., 29
organized crime, 22, 24–25, 27, 98
outer space, 22, 36–37, 80, 151, 178, 180–186, 190
Outer Space Act, 22, 80, 190

Pace, Frank, 154
parity support farm program, 153–158
Parliament, British, 6
Pendergast, Thomas J., 27, 55, 176
Pepper, Claude, 72
Pittman, Key, 69–70
prayer in public schools, 189, 206, 211–212
Profiles in Courage (Kennedy), 28
public housing, 107–110
public power, 177

Rayburn, Sam, 17, 164, 169–170, 175
Reagan, Ronald, 204, 205–206
Reed, Daniel, 86–87
Republican-Southern Democratic coalition, 49–50, 51, 96, 99, 105–106, 108, 111, 113–118, 119, 123, 124, 127, 128, 151
Reynolds, Robert Rice, 141
Robinson, Joe, 114
Roosevelt, Eleanor, 118
Roosevelt, Franklin D., 8, 10, 27, 54, 67, 68, 68, 70, 83, 100–101, 103–104, 114, 115, 117–118, 119, 153, 176, 194
rural electrification, 50
Russell, Richard B., 13–15, 22, 31–32, 58–59, 86, 89–94, 96, 105, 106–107, 112, 127, 132, 147, 182, 183, 191, 192

Schlesinger, Arthur, Jr., 29
Selective Service Act, 71
Senate Democratic Policy Committee, 11–12, 15, 17, 77, 78, 132, 133
Shivers, Allan, 163, 168, 170–171, 172
Smathers, George, 28
Smith, Cotton Ed, 115
Smith, Alfred E., 32, 117
socialized medicine, 82–83
social legislation, 23, 73, 80, 114, 147, 177, 186, 189, 200, 205, 206–207, 211–212
social services, 206–207
South Africa, 121
Southern Manifesto, 107

Soviet Union, 36, 37, 51, 57, 74–75, 78–79, 180–181, 183, 184–185
space program, 22, 36–37, 80, 151, 178, 180–186, 190
Spanish civil war, 56, 68
Sputnik, 36
Stalin, Josef, 57
Stennis, John C., 18, 123
Stevenson, Adlai, 27, 62, 63, 171, 172
Subversive Activities Control Act, 150, 151
Supreme Court reorganization bill, 115
Symington, Stuart, 98, 160, 162, 188

Taft, Robert A., 78, 79, 94–97, 102–103, 105, 116, 125, 148, 149, 173, 175
Taft-Hartley Labor Relations Act, 29–30, 150–151
Tammany Hall, 26, 115, 119, 176
Teapot Dome scandal, 87
Teller, Edward, 36, 183–184
Thompson, William Hale (Big Bill the Builder), 141
tidelands issue, 46, 163–165, 166
Tobey, Charles, 8
Truman, Harry S, 14, 26–27, 48, 54–55, 57, 58–62, 74, 75, 76, 95, 101, 150, 153, 155, 176
Twilight of the Presidency, The (Reedy), 2
two-term Constitutional amendment, 151, 173, 177
Tydings, Millard, 139, 142

U.N. Genocide Convention, 75–76, 79
U.N. Human Rights Covenant, 75, 79, 82

Vandenberg, Arthur, 69–70, 75

Vietnam, 98, 198–199

Wallace, Henry A., 92
Washington, George, 65, 66
Weisl, Edwin, 183
Wheeler, Burton K., 65

White, Harry Dexter, 75
Wilson, Charles, 131
Wilson, Woodrow, 6, 13, 44, 66
Wofford, Harris, 29
World War II neutrality issue, 67–71